Cambridge Elements ≡

Elements in the Philosophy of Biology
edited by
Grant Ramsey
KU Leuven
Michael Ruse
Florida State University

SLIME MOULD AND PHILOSOPHY

Matthew Sims
Ruhr-Universität Bochum

Shaftesbury Road, Cambridge CB2 8EA, United Kingdom

One Liberty Plaza, 20th Floor, New York, NY 10006, USA

477 Williamstown Road, Port Melbourne, VIC 3207, Australia

314–321, 3rd Floor, Plot 3, Splendor Forum, Jasola District Centre,
New Delhi – 110025, India

103 Penang Road, #05–06/07, Visioncrest Commercial, Singapore 238467

Cambridge University Press is part of Cambridge University Press & Assessment,
a department of the University of Cambridge.

We share the University's mission to contribute to society through the pursuit of
education, learning and research at the highest international levels of excellence.

www.cambridge.org
Information on this title: www.cambridge.org/9781009488624

DOI: 10.1017/9781009488648

When citing this work, please include a reference to the DOI 10.1017/9781009488648

First published 2024

A catalogue record for this publication is available from the British Library

ISBN 978-1-009-48862-4 Hardback
ISBN 978-1-009-48861-7 Paperback
ISSN 2515-1126 (online)
ISSN 2515-1118 (print)

Additional resources for this publication at www.cambridge.org/Sims

Slime Mould and Philosophy

Elements in the Philosophy of Biology

DOI: 10.1017/9781009488648
First published online: December 2024

Matthew Sims
Ruhr-Universität Bochum

Author for correspondence: Matthew Sims,
matthew.sims-m4e@ruhr-uni-bochum.de

Abstract: *Physarum polycephalum*, also known more colloquially as 'the blob', 'acellular slime mould', or just 'slime mould', is a unicellular multinucleate protist that has continued to attract the interest of biologists over the past century because of its complex life cycle, unique physiology, morphology, and behaviour. More recently, attention has shifted to Physarum as a model organism for investigating putative cognitive capacities such as decision making, learning, and memory in organisms without nervous systems. The aim of this Element is to illustrate how Physarum can be used as a valuable tool for approaching various topics in the philosophy of biology. Physarum and its behaviour not only pose a challenge to some of the received views of biological processes but also, I shall argue, provide an opportunity to clarify and appropriately sharpen the concepts underlying such received views.

Keywords: slime mould, philosophy of biology, niche construction, biological individuality, non-neuronal memory

ISBNs: 9781009488624 (HB), 9781009488617 (PB), 9781009488648 (OC)
ISSNs: 2515-1126 (online), 2515-1118 (print)

Contents

1 Introduction

Physarum polycephalum (henceforth Physarum), also known more colloquially as 'the blob', 'acellular slime mould', or simply 'slime mould', is a unicellular protist that has continued to attract the interest of biologists over the past century because of its complex life cycle, unique physiology, morphology, and behaviour. It has been used as a model organism for numerous studies, some of which include the investigation of various mechanisms that underpin synchronous nuclear division, the development of drugs for the treatment of cancerous tumours, and the investigation of putative cognitive capacities such as decision making, learning, and memory in organisms that lack nervous systems. More recently, biologists have even used Physarum to study the effects of microgravity on growth and behaviour in outer space.

Although Physarum has much to offer in terms of being a model organism for biological research, as the non-exhaustive list of uses above should make apparent, the aim of this Element is to illustrate how Physarum can be a valuable *tool* for approaching various issues in the philosophy of biology. Physarum's unique features not only pose a challenge to some of the received views of biological processes but also, I shall argue, provide an opportunity to clarify and appropriately sharpen the concepts underlying such received views. For example, the notion of 'niche construction' has become an important – yet not fully agreed upon – concept within the context of evolutionary biology. Roughly, niche construction refers to the idea that evolution is influenced not only by how (genetic) variation allows organisms to differentially adapt to the challenges of their environment but also by how organisms modify their environments and thus alter which selection pressures they are exposed to. By looking closely at Physarum's complex life cycle, an opportunity arises to understand how different kinds of niche construction are exemplified and, more generally, how those different kinds of niche construction often dynamically interact.

Each section of this Element is organised around a distinct philosophical issue as contextualised by Physarum. Using Physarum's life cycle as a concrete example, Section 2 focuses on the issue of how attention to complex life cycles can provide insights into the intricacies of niche construction. Section 3 addresses the tension between the idea that metabolic exchange is a necessary feature of all known life and the fact that biologists classify spores as a form of life despite their being metabolically inert for long periods of time. Section 4 turns to a central concept in biology – 'biological individuality' – and how Physarum's fragmentation and fusion behaviour forces us to rethink at least one way of understanding that concept. Lastly, Section 5 turns to the issue of whether to understand

Physarum's use of its extracellular slime trails as a form of memory – and if so whether such memory is subject to explanation in terms of cognition.

In addition to providing a context for investigating various concepts and puzzling issues in the philosophy of biology, the abundance of empirical research on Physarum provides a rich resource for constraining how such issues might be addressed. This is, however, not to say that these issues can be addressed without philosophically getting one's hands dirty – they cannot. One additional important aspect of using Physarum as a tool to approach difficult questions regarding niche construction, biological individuality, and cognition in non-neuronal organisms is that many answers can be used to generate testable hypotheses. In other words, although philosophising is a necessary step in addressing many of these issues, it is not the only or the last step.

Although I will argue that certain ways of addressing the focal issues brought to the fore in this Element are more plausible than others, the conceptual revisions proposed, and conclusions drawn by no means represent anything like a final word – they are tentative in that they can be both revised and/or overturned on the basis of further empirical evidence. This kind of openness to empirical amenability should not be seen as a defect but should rather be seen as an instance of how philosophy and biology are a mutually guiding endeavour; an empirically informed philosophy may be used to generate testable hypotheses and the results of such hypothesis testing should feed back into altering the very philosophical accounts which generated the initial hypotheses. This may be seen as an instance of what Pradeu et al. (2021) have called 'philosophy in science' as opposed to 'philosophy on science'. By throwing into relief some perplexing issues in the philosophy of biology that *P. polycephalum* both raises and can be used to investigate, this Element serves as both an illustration of how this outlier model organism can be used as a tool for the philosophy of biology, and an invitation for both philosophers and biologists to do so. Although the aim of this Element is not to provide a sustained argument for one particular philosophical issue, one might extrapolate from the useful role that Physarum is shown to play in each section to the more general claim that advancing the philosophy of biology requires investigating both typical and atypical model organisms. Concepts and theories based exclusively on the former may be more intuitive but less representative of the incredible diversity found in the biological world.

A few preliminary remarks: each section of this Element begins with some background information that frames the issue at hand and then unpacks the various details required to grapple with the issue. Given the nature of this Element – a book centred upon the philosophy of biology – many of the details will involve both biological descriptions and theoretical concepts: the arsenal of philosophers of biology. I will do my best, however, to avoid bogging the reader down with any unnecessary details for fear of not seeing the forest for the trees. There are also a fair number of figures throughout the Element. These are intended to supplement some of the more abstract concepts and descriptions that are introduced in each section. They are by no means intended as replacements for the text.

I have personally been fascinated – unabashedly so – by Physarum and its behaviour for some years now and I hope this Element can also serve to awaken a level of fascination for Physarum in both readers who are familiar and those who are unfamiliar with this organism that is at least on par with my own.

1.1 What Is *P. polycephalum*?

In order to understand how to use Physarum as a tool, it is important to firstly have a general understanding of what the proposed tool is. *P. polycephalum* is an amoebozoan protist belonging to the class myxomycetes (i.e., the 'acellular slime moulds' or 'true slime moulds') (Stephenson and Stempen, 1994) (see Table 1).

It is a eukaryote (i.e., having a nucleus and other membrane-bound organelles), and like other myxomycetes members, Physarum remains unicellular over the course of its whole life cycle, developing from an uninucleate cell into a multinucleate unicellular mass – a 'plasmodium'.[1] In this life cycle stage transition, Physarum goes from being a microorganism to a bright yellow, giant cell that is visible with the naked eye (see Figure 1). A species with a broad geographic distribution, Physarum lives in wooded areas, taking up residence in/on dead tree stumps and logs that offer the shade, cool temperature, and moisture it needs to survive. Physarum's diet consists of living microorganisms such as

Table 1 Taxonomic classification of *P. polycephalum*

Domain	Eukaryota
Kingdom	Protista
Phylum	Amoebozoa
Class	Myxomycetes
Order	Physarales
Family	Physaraceae
Genus	*Physarum*
Species	*P. polycephalum*

---

[1] Acellular slime moulds should not be confused with cellular slime moulds of the class *Dictyostelia* (e.g., *Dictyostelium discoideum*). The latter are social amoeba that aggregate at a stage in their life cycle, forming a multicellular vegetative slug.

Figure 1 *P. polycephalum* plasmodium: a giant, yellow, unicellular mass on a log. (Credit: Rich Hoyer. https://creativecommons.org/licenses/by-sa/3.0/. Unaltered photo). The colour version of this figure is available at www.cambridge.org/Sims

bacteria, yeast, amoeba, and also decomposing organic matter. Small spore-eating beetle species, woodlice, land slugs, and other myxomycetes species are among Physarum's predators (and more broadly, the predators of myxomycetes).

Physarum – in its plasmodial stage – has proven to be easy to culture in labs under conditions roughly mimicking those in which it thrives in the wild. This entails being kept in a humid and dark enclosure and having a steady food supply – usually store-bought dried oats. In addition to its unique features, the ease with which Physarum is cultured has added to its popularity as a model organism.

Having a basic understanding of what Physarum is, let us without further ado put this fascinating organism to work.

2 Niche Construction and Complex Life Cycles

According to Darwinian evolution by natural selection, whether some phenotypes (i.e., observable traits) are selected for and as a result spread through a population over time is largely determined by how well those phenotypes allow individual organisms to cope with environmental selection pressures they encounter (e.g., predation, changes in food availability, changes in exposure to physical stressors, etc.). Different kinds of niche construction may be understood roughly as distinct ways that organisms systematically affect the selection pressures that they, their offspring, and/or cohabitants face. Since whether some phenotypes evolve in a population is at least partly a response to selection pressures *as affected by niche construction*, understanding different kinds of niche construction is required for a more complete account of evolution by natural selection. This presumably involves not only understanding how each kind of niche construction is exemplified in isolation (an abstraction) but also understanding how different kinds of niche construction interact over time in broader natural contexts.

Using Physarum's complex life cycle as one such context, the aim of this section is to investigate different kinds of niche construction and to identify some of the ways that they are causally related. The broader perspective that niche construction brings into focus is how organisms not only plastically adapt to their environments but by doing so also modify their relation to environmental selective pressures in ways that can potentially affect their own evolution, and/or the evolution of other taxa which they regularly interact with. By investigating Physarum's different life cycle stages and the transitions between them through the lens of niche construction, the emphasis is placed upon how those stages, given variation in specific phenotypic parameter values, can go onto influence evolutionary dynamics *and* are quite possibly the outcomes of prior niche construction and ongoing evolutionary dynamics. My aim in this section is not to speculate about any particular role that a form of niche construction has played in Physarum's evolutionary history; rather, it is to exhume the differential importance of different kinds of niche construction and their causally interweaving relations that are specific to different stages of Physarum's complex life cycle. In doing so, this section provides an impetus for future investigation and modelling of the evolutionary dynamics associated with the different kinds of niche construction and their relative significance to the stages of Physarum's complex life cycle.

I will firstly discuss the concept of niche construction and what it was initially a response to. I shall then look at the three kinds of niche construction proposed by Aaby and Ramsey (2019) as a manner of expanding the categories of canonical niche construction theory. After articulating the notion of complex life cycles, I will then describe the details of Physarum's complex multigenerational life cycle. Lastly, I will turn to the task of identifying both the different kinds of niche construction as they arise in the various stages of Physarum's complex life cycle and how those different kinds of niche construction often dynamically interact between and within various life cycle stages.

2.1 Niche Construction: An Overview

Beavers use mud, stones, and tree branches to build dams in rivers. This seems to be common knowledge. However, what are the implications of building dams for the evolution of those large rodents we know as beavers? By constructing dams, beavers create small, controlled aquatic pools in which they can easily access primary food sources and nest. The behaviour of dam-building has been so effective in contributing to the beaver's fitness (i.e., survival and fecundity) that this behavioural phenotype has become characteristic of beavers.[2] Moreover, and importantly, at some point in their evolutionary history beavers developed other phenotypes that made aquatic life and dam building easier: webbed feet and a flat, mud-packing tail. In other words, beavers have modified their physical environments in ways that have affected the impact of selection pressures upon them, and this in turn has affected which phenotypes have been selected for. Dam construction on the part of beavers is a paradigm example of niche construction (or at least one type of it as we shall soon see).

Niche construction is 'the process whereby organisms, through their metabolism, their activities, and their choices, modify their own and/or each other's niches' (Odling-Smee et al., 2003: 419). From an evolutionary perspective, *niches* may be construed as the collection of all selection pressures that populations regularly encounter (Odling-Smee et al., 2003). Niche construction thus describes how organisms affect their own (and other's) evolution. This kind of approach to evolutionary explanation may be contrasted to those that are known as 'externalist explanations' (Lewontin, 1983) (see also Godfrey-Smith, 1996). Externalist explanations, it is argued, are founded on the supposition that evolutionary change is solely an adaptive response to environmental challenges – a supposition that has found its way in much of neo-Darwinian evolutionary thinking. These explanations emphasise organismal evolution as a function of the organism and the environment while simultaneously relegating the environment to a background condition. The environment, in other words, is viewed as something that is not affected by the organism in any way that is relevant to evolution.

Departing from explanatory externalism, niche construction stresses the idea that organisms are active causes of their own evolution.[3] Whether it is beavers modifying their river habitats by constructing dams, burrowing worms altering the composition of the soil in which they live, or trees shedding leaves and modifying the soil substrate around them, organisms routinely affect their selective environment. To this, proponents of niche construction view inheritance as something that outstrips mere genetic inheritance (i.e., the transmission of DNA across parent–offspring lineages or through bacterial DNA exchange),

---

[2] I will continue to use the term 'fitness' to refer to the combination of viability and fecundity, following the convention of how the term is understood in life history.

[3] Some of the key figures in biology and ecology that laid the groundwork for the development of niche construction theory were Darwin (1881), Clements (1916), Schrödinger (1944), and Waddington (1969).

acknowledging what is called 'ecological inheritance'. This refers to 'the modified environmental states that niche-constructing organisms bequeath to their descendants' (Scott-Phillips et al., 2014: 1233). In acknowledging the importance of the organism's impàct upon evolution, the niche construction approach has been viewed as a manner of supplementing standard evolutionary theory, offering a more complete evolutionary explanation than externalist explanations can provide alone (Odling-Smee et al., 2003).

Canonical niche construction theory (Laland et al., 2000; Odling-Smee et al., 2003) recognises two ways that organisms can construct their niches: 'perturbation', occurs when organisms modify their physical environment (think of the beaver and its dam-building); and 'relocation', occurs when organisms modify their spatio-temporal relation to the selective environment (think of birds that migrate every winter to warmer climates to avoid freezing and/or starvation). More recently, Bendik Hellem Aaby and Grant Ramsey (2019) have put forth a tripartite niche construction taxonomy, expanding these two niche construction categories.[4] Although the scope of this section does not permit a detailed treatment of their arguments, a brief description should serve to make explicit their rationale for developing the kind of tripartite taxonomy that they put forth.

Firstly, Aaby and Ramsey note that organisms not only relocate to accommodate changing resource conditions (e.g., temperature, food, predators, etc.) but they also often physically change their spatio-temporal relation to other organisms to maintain and control the flow of information between them. For instance, an antelope might follow a nearby lion in order to remain informed of its potential predator's location, thereby reducing its uncertainty about an attack. This kind of relational modification, although having something in common with relocation, is not covered by it; it is an indirect epistemic pay-off that the antelope's change of spatial location in relation to the lion affords and not a direct pay-off of escape. Thus, the first line of reasoning motivates a broadening of the relocation category.

Aaby and Ramsey's second line of reasoning for an expansion is based upon the idea that in order for canonical niche construction theory to be consistent with the notion of niche that it adopts from Odling-Smee et al. (2003), a third kind of niche construction must be acknowledged. Odling-Smee et al. (2003), in developing the niche construction approach, deploy Walter J. Bock's (1980) *factor–feature interactions* analysis of niche. According to this analysis, 'factors' are selection pressures and 'features' are organismal phenotypes. If a niche consists of the sum of all selection pressures faced by a population, then

---

[4] Also see (Sultan, 2015) and (Chiu, 2019) for similar efforts to expand the categories of canonical niche construction theory.

this is just to say that a niche consists of the sum of factors faced by a population that select for organismal features. If something like this is assumed correct, which it is by canonical niche construction theory, then organisms can alter their niche in three ways: (1) modifying factors (i.e., perturbation), (2) modifying the relation between factors and features (e.g., relocation), and (3) modifying their own features. Thus, for niche construction to be consistent with the *factor–feature interactions* conception of niche, *constitutive modifications* to the features of the organism must be taken on as a third category of niche construction.

2.2 Three Kinds of Niche Construction

Aaby and Ramsey refer to the various ways (1–3 in the previous paragraph) that factor–feature relations can be modified, respectively, *as external niche construction, relational niche construction, and constitutive niche construction*. External niche construction (ENC) refers to the modification of the biotic and abiotic environmental factors made by a focal organism, which thereby changes its selective environment, that of its offspring, and/or cohabitants. ENC is equivalent to perturbation of canonical niche construction theory. Paradigmatic examples of ENC include the construction of dams by beavers or the construction of nests by birds. Relational niche construction (RNC) refers to the modification of a focal organism's spatio-temporal location relative to environmental factors but also the modification in relation to other organisms which alter a focal organism's epistemic niche. This latter kind of modification – amongst other things – allows for the maintenance of information flow from one organism to another and is particularly crucial for organised social behaviour that is structured according to a division of labour (Sterelny, 2003). Thus, RNC conceptually includes relocation but represents a broader category than relocation.

Lastly, constitutive niche construction (CNC) refers to the modification of a focal organism's features that alter its causal relation(s) to environmental factors, and thus alters its (or its offspring and/or cohabitants) relation to selection pressures.[5] CNC occurs via the mechanism of phenotypic plasticity – environmentally induced, non-heritable trait modifications that include reversible and nonreversible behavioural and morphological changes.[6] For instance, a plant, being sessile, cannot move to a different location if deprived of light. Instead, it will modify the effects of environmental factors by way of phenotypically plastic responses, sometimes drastically changing its morphology. This might include growing broader leaves to compensate for less light or growing narrower leaves to

---

[5] Similar to CNC, the notion of 'experiential niche construction' has been extensively developed by Sultan (2015).

[6] Epigenetic modifications are recognised as one of the key molecular mechanisms contributing to phenotypic plasticity (see Bateson and Gluckman, 2011).

compensate for exposure to excess light (Sultan, 2015). Importantly, such differences in leaf shape amongst members of the same species are not due to genetic differences; they are different environmentally induced forms that genetically identical plants (or the same plant) may take over the course of their (its) development.

Some proponents of niche construction have expressed scepticism regarding such an expansion (see Godfrey-Smith, 1996, 2001; Baedke et al., 2021; Trappes et al., 2022). Part of such scepticism may be seen as stemming from a general worry concerning the ubiquity of niche construction, namely: if every selection-relevant biotic or environmental modification that an organism makes is a form of niche construction, then the concept becomes trivial and of no explanatory use. Discussing and responding to this criticism, Abby and Ramsey remind us that both selection and genetic drift are equally ubiquitous phenomena and that this case does not make them any less useful. Their usefulness in evolutionary theory stems from recognising that not every instance of selection or drift is equally important in every evolutionary process. That is, there are explanatory contexts in which specific forms of selection or drift should be foregrounded, whilst others are backgrounded and this differential importance across different contexts allows selection and drift to remain useful notions. According to Abby and Ramsey, niche construction is similar in this manner. Despite niche construction's ubiquity, the differential importance of different types of niche construction relative to a particular explanatory context can help us to understand and model evolutionary processes. In one particular stage that makes up Physarum's complex life cycle (or transitions to and/or from that stage), a number of different types of niche construction are possibly at play. However, understanding the differential importance of ENC, RNC, CNC, or any combination thereof relative to that stage can be useful in understanding (and informing models of) the evolutionary dynamics that have stabilised that stage within the sequence of stages that make up Physarum's life cycle.[7]

Another worry that some sceptics have raised has to do with the idea that describing a plastic response in terms of something like CNC fails to provide any additional information about that response and, thus, to do so is unwarranted. This worry, however, overlooks the fact that although phenotypic plasticity is a mechanism that underwrites niche construction, considering the evolutionary consequences of plastic responses is extrinsic to any accurate description of a response as such. Describing some variable response as a form of phenotypic plasticity is to acknowledge that it is a change in phenotype in response to an environmental or internal cue without any accompanying

---

[7] I would like to thank an anonymous reviewer for pushing me to clarify this point.

genetic change. Although there have been various suggestions that such responses can have evolutionary impacts on the subsequent genetic fixation of those phenotypes (West-Eberhard, 2003; Bateson and Gluckman, 2011; Levis and Pfennig, 2016), that this is the case is above and beyond describing some response as an instance of phenotypic plasticity. The notion of niche construction, on the other hand, was formulated in the context of evolutionary theory. Thus, describing some plastic response as niche construction embeds it in a broader evolutionary context in which the historical, ongoing, or future consequences of that response upon evolutionary dynamics is central.

In what follows, I will assume expanding niche construction to include more than perturbance and relocation is theoretically warranted, enough so to justify the further exploration of Aaby and Ramsey's tripartite niche construction taxonomy. One manner of examining the details of each of the three kinds of niche construction is to look at how they occur within a life cycle of one organism. Looking at particular complex life cycles in which all three kinds of niche construction are present, I shall argue, provides a broad perspective for examining the details of ENC, RNC, and CNC and the part that each plays in altering the selective environment of a focal organism. This of course raises the question of what a complex life cycle is, a topic to which we will now turn.

2.3 Complex Life Cycles

Biologists often explore life cycles to understand the variety of developmental and reproductive processes that occur from one stage in a generation (such as a zygote, spore, or larva) to the same stage in the next generation of a particular species. A 'life cycle' is a 'series of organisational transformations and reproductive phases that lead from a given stage of development of the same organisational form, to the same stage of development of the same organisational form in a following generation, through all organisational forms of the organism' (Fusco and Minelli, 2019: 23). An organisational form refers to a distinct type of entity that has its own ontogeny and thus represents a single generation that undergoes development (Fusco and Minelli, 2019). The life cycle of, say, a human or an earthworm has a single organisational form that, through a sequence of developmental processes, is repeated after one generation. The same is true of metamorphosing beetles and butterflies despite the fact that the development of a single organisational form consists of various stages with drastically different phenotypes (the egg, larva, pupa, and adult). Not all life cycles involve only one organisational form though.

One general feature that biologists use to pick out complex life cycles is *alternation of generations* (Fusco and Minelli, 2019). Alternation of generations refers to a life cycle pattern in which there is an alternation between at least two different organisational forms with different ploidy levels (haploid or diploid), each of which also often displays notable differences in morphology, behaviour, and physiology. Within such a multigenerational life cycle, one generation produces another with a distinct organisational form, which in turn produces the next generation of the first type again, marking a return to the beginning of the life cycle of a different token organism. In this context, production can be understood as a causal relation (Godfrey-Smith, 2016) in which one entity brings another entity into existence. This can be contrasted with developing, which is a continuation or progression from an existing stage, rather than a causal relation.

Alternation of generations is clearly exemplified by plants such as ferns, mosses, and some algae whose complex life cycles alternate generationally between two organisational forms: one being a sex cell-producing plant that has a single set of chromosomes (a haploid gametophyte) and the other a spore-producing plant with two sets of chromosomes (a diploid sporophyte).[8] Each of these forms represents a distinct generation with its own development and each organisational form produces the other. In contrast, more recently evolved animal lineages, including humans and other mammals, exhibit simple, mono-generational life cycles. Although mammalian reproduction involves haploid and diploid stages, the haploid stage is limited to gametes (egg or sperm cells) and does not have its own ontogeny. Thus, neither egg nor sperm qualify as a separate generation. Through sexual reproduction – more specifically fertil-isation – adult mammals give rise to a diploid zygote, marking a new gener-ation. This zygote develops into a diploid adult, resembling its parents. To stress, haploid mammalian sex cells do not produce the zygote; rather, the reproducing parents produce the zygote. Nor does the zygote produce the adult; it develops into an adult.[9] In a mammalian life cycle, there is only one organisational form that develops and gives rise to the same organisational form of a distinct generation, starting the life cycle anew.

One fascinating example of a complex life cycle, which offers valuable insights into understanding ENC, RNC, and CNC, and also exemplifies the potential value of investigating complex life cycles for the purposes of under-standing niche construction, is that of *P. polycephalum*. The life cycle of Physarum involves two vegetative stages, or periods in which there is feeding, growth, and cellular repair. These stages are the uninucleate 'ameboflagellate stage' and the multinucleate 'plasmodial stage'. Both stages exhibit distinct organisational forms and have different ploidy levels (haploid or diploid).

---

[8] For numerous examples, see Fusco and Minelli (2019).

[9] The same can be said of complete metamorphosing beetles and sea urchins; a larva in such a case does not produce an adult but develops into one.

Alternation of generations is apparent in Physarum's life cycle as ameboflagellates and plasmodia produce each other through characteristic pathways (Gorman and Wilkins, 1980). This multigenerational haplodiplontic life cycle features alternating generations of these two vegetative stages.

In addition to these two vegetative stages, Physarum's life cycle also includes three dormant stages: 'the microcyst stage', 'the sclerotium stage', and 'the spore stage'. Of these three, only the third is irreversible and represents a non-optional developmental transition between the plasmodium and ameboflagellate. Lastly, there is an obligate and non-reversible 'fruiting body stage' which leads to the spore stage.

I will now briefly describe the journey of *P. polycephalum* through each of its life cycle stages, beginning with the spore and ending with the formation of the spore. I have tried to keep these descriptions brief and to the point; however, there is a certain level of detail that is required to convey the diverse characteristics of life cycle stages of an organism like Physarum. These details play a crucial role in assessing which (if any) of the three different kinds of niche construction are present in the various stages. I have included Figure 2 as visual reference. Both the following descriptions and Figure 2 may be revisited while progressing through the remaining pages of this Element for the purpose of regaining one's bearing.

2.4 Stages of Physarum's Complex Life Cycle

Physarum **spores** are microscopic dispersal units, consisting of a single haploid nucleus enclosed within a resistant wall. Separating Physarum's two vegetative stages, spores represent a dormant (i.e., metabolically inert) stage that may stay viable for several years in unfavourable conditions such as drought or cold. When favourable conditions resume, a spore germinates, producing an ameboflagellate cell. The fact that an organisational form distinct from the sporulating plasmodium (the ameboflagellate) hatches after germination is what makes the spore an irreversible dormant stage.

The **ameboflagellate** stage refers to either of two microscopic haploid cell forms representing the uninucleate vegetative stage of Physarum's life cycle. These are the **'myxamoeba'** and the **'biflagellate'** forms. As their names suggest, the former is an amoeboid cell with no fixed shape, while the latter is an elongated cell with two flagella of different lengths (i.e., hair-like appendages that are used for swimming). If spore germination occurs on a surface with less water content, the result will be a myxamoeba cell. However, when spore germination occurs in free water, this results in the hatching of a biflagellate cell (Clark and Haskins, 2016).

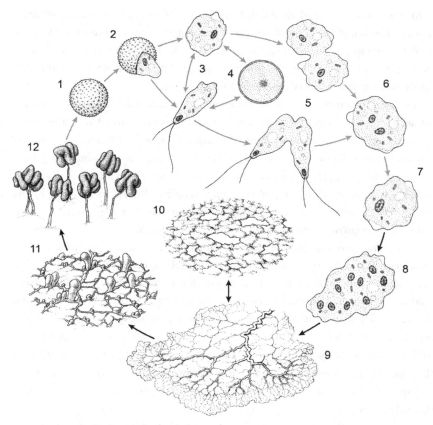

Figure 2 Stages of *P. polycephalum's* complex life cycle: (1) spore;
(2) germinating spore; (3) ameboflagellate: myxamoeba above and biflagellate
below; (4) microcyst; (5) ameboflagellate fusion: myxamoeba fusion on the
right and biflagellate fusion on the left; (6) fused cells prior to nuclear fusion;
(7) nuclear fusion; (8) early plasmodial cell after nuclear mitosis without
cell division; (9) mature plasmodium; (10) sclerotium; (11) commitment to
fruiting stage; (12) fruiting bodies. Haploid and diploid stages indicated by grey
arrows and black arrows, respectively. Illustration by Guido I. Prieto
(2024) adapted from Stephenson and Stempen (1994).

Myxamoebae locomote on surfaces by pulling and pushing themselves with
temporary, arm-like projections called 'pseudopods'. They feed upon fungal
spores, bacteria, and other microorganisms via phagocytosis and reproduce through
binary fission (Clark and Haskins, 2015). During division, however, myxamoebae
cannot feed (Collins, 1979). Successive divisions result in a colony of genetic
clones. If a myxamoeba becomes submerged in free water, it rapidly transforms

into a swimming, biflagellate cell. Biflagellates may feed but cannot undergo binary fission (Clark and Haskins, 2015). Upon encountering drier conditions, the biflagellate will rapidly revert into a myxamoeba again. This highly plastic cell transformation can occur multiple times in either direction, depending upon the availability of free water (Pagh and Adelman, 1988).

Under unfavourable conditions such as starvation, drought, overabundance of water, and overcrowding, the ameboflagellate may convert into a dormant **microcyst**. This resistant structure, a suspension of vegetative growth, can remain viable for long periods of time. Encysting of the ameboflagellate involves the synthesis of a resistant wall around the cell, in addition to various other intracellular changes (Gorman and Wilkins, 1980). In contrast to the spore, the microcyst is a reversable dormant stage; when environmental conditions improve, it reverts into ameboflagellate again.

Upon encountering another mating competent cell of a compatible mating type, two haploid myxamoebae (or two biflagellate cells) may sexually fuse. This leads to the initiation of the **plasmodium** stage, in which nuclear fusion and the subsequent formation of a diploid zygote cell occur. As the diploid nucleus undergoes multiple rounds of division without cell division, the cell grows and develops into a multinucleate plasmodium, the other vegetative stage of Physarum's life cycle. It is during this stage that Physarum becomes visible to the naked eye as a mass of bright yellow, slimy protoplasm. It may reach a size of up to 900 cm^2 and can crawl across surfaces at a speed of up to 5 cm/h (Kessler, 1982).

As it grows, the plasmodium migrates across decaying organic substrates, feeding and avoiding any environmental conditions that may challenge its viability. Plasmodia consume bacteria, fungi, and other microbes (including other myxomycete amoebae), but can also feed on non-living organic matter. Feeding occurs in this stage via both phagocytosis and the excretion of enzymes that break down organic matter which is then absorbed into the cell (Bailey, 1997). The cell's shape is plastically reorganised on the go via the restructuring of an internal, vein-like tubular network, through which protoplasm is rhythmically shuttled. Such shuttling pushes the edges of the cell towards food or away from potentially harmful substances. As it migrates, a trail of extracellular slime (i.e., a non-living, cytoplasmic casing) is secreted which, amongst other things, functions as a lubricating surface upon which to crawl more easily (Patino-Ramirez et al., 2019). Upon encountering a patch where nutrient conditions are adequate, plasmodium may remain sedentary, growing steadily at that location (Dussutour et al., 2010).

When encountering adverse conditions such as prolonged periods of drought, starvation, and/or low temperatures, a plasmodium may transform into a dried, hard, resistant mass called the '**sclerotium**' (plural: sclerotia). Like the micro-cyst, the sclerotium represents a reversible dormant structure, the formation of which allows a plasmodium to withstand unfavourable growth and metabolic conditions until those conditions subside. A plasmodium can remain dormant as sclerotium anywhere from months to years (Sperry et al., 2022). When condi-tions improve, the sclerotium may revert back into a plasmodium and continue living as a large diploid vegetative cell. Like the microcyst, the sclerotium is also an optional developmental stage; whether it occurs in an individual Physarum's life cycle will depend upon the kinds of environmental conditions which are encountered by the individual plasmodium.

Within a period of extended starvation, a mature plasmodium will migrate from its usual shaded microhabitat into the light, where various biochemical events lead to the differentiation of the cell protoplasm into multiple fruiting bodies or '**sporangia**' (singular: sporangium) (Gorman and Wilkins, 1980). Physarum's sporangia consist of long, thin, twisted stalks upon which multiheaded spore enclosures are attached: hence the species name 'polycephalum' (many-headed). Once the process of fruiting has begun, it is irreversible. During spore develop-ment, meiotic cell division occurs, resulting in the formation of multiple uni-nucleate spores within the spore enclosure. After a period in which fruiting bodies and their spore contents dry, spores are released and dispersed by wind or also sometimes via surface contact with spore-eating arthropods (Blackwell, 1984; Sugiura et al., 2019). This completes Physarum's complex life cycle.

How might the various stages of Physarum's life cycle provide concrete examples of either ENC, RNC, or CNC, and how might these forms of niche construction work in tandem? This is the topic to which we will now turn.

2.5 Three Kinds of Niche Construction Exemplified in Physarum's Life Cycle

Recall, Aaby and Ramsey's tripartite niche construction taxonomy: ENC is the modification of an organism's environmental factors; RNC is the modification of an organism's spatio-temporal relation to environmental factors and other organisms; CNC is the modification of an organism's features that alter its causal relation(s) to environmental factors. Importantly, ENC, RNC, and CNC are forms of niche construction because an organism's engaging in any of them may influence the impact of selection pressures and hence affect fitness and evolution. Now let's consider how these various kinds of niche construction may figure into some of the stages of Physarum's life cycle. I will focus upon Physarum's two vegetative stages – optional dormant stages, and the fruiting body stage – because I find them to be the most revealing in terms of how

ENC, RNC, and CNC interact across development. The examples of niche construction that I identify here are not meant in any way to be exhaustive; within the various stages of Physarum's life cycle there are undoubtedly many more instances of niche construction that occur. For reasons of space, I cannot deal with all of them here.

Starting with the reversible and optional transformation from myxamoeba to biflagellate, I would like to argue that this transformation provides an example of both CNC and RNC. To see this, consider that a myxamoeba is limited to the use of pseudopods for locomotion and hence cannot swim (or at least cannot swim effectively). As such, the presence of free water introduces a fitness-relevant challenge: assuming that capturing food in water requires effective locomotion, a submerged myxamoeba may be less successful at capturing food than it would be in a non-water microhabitat. The ability to transform into a biflagellate mediates this challenge. Although the degree that a biflagellate cell can direct its movement is very limited and the distance that it can swim is typically short, being able to swim can improve feeding in some situations (Clark and Haskins, 2015). In morphologically transforming from a myxamoeba to a swimming biflagellate, the ameboflagellate increases the amount of food available to it while it is in its water microhabitat. Moreover, because biflagellate cells cannot undergo binary fission, and feeding cannot occur at the same time as binary fission, a biflagellate may continue to feed without interruption as long as food is available. In short, the water-induced transformation from myxamoeba to biflagellate is an active modification of the ameboflagellate's features that change its causal relation(s) to environmental factors. This is a clear instance of CNC, one that albeit occurs in a motile organism.

The transformation into a biflagellate, however, comes with a potential fitness cost since of the two ameboflagellate forms only the myxamoeba can undergo binary fission and produce daughter cells. As such, a sustained existence as a biflagellate means low ameboflagellate fecundity. Transforming into a biflagellate thus seems to mediate one kind of selection pressure but in turn introduces another: the inability to reproduce as a biflagellate cell. One manner of accommodating this morphology-related decline in fitness is for the ameboflagellate to swim to a dry surface (if the surface is not too far away), thus changing its spatial relation to the water microhabitat that induced its current form. This active change in location on the part of the ameboflagellate represents an instance of RNC, which in addition to the subsequent reversion to the myxamoeba form – an instance of CNC – re-establishes the ameboflagellate's ability to undergo binary fission again.

The transformation from myxamoeba to biflagellate and back exemplifies not only CNC and RNC but also an interesting way that these two kinds of niche construction are related: CNC may allow an organism to temporarily compensate for the effects of changing environmental factors via plastic phenotypic modification (e.g., transforming into a biflagellate swimming cell and as a result being able to capture more food) *and* in some cases, the same CNC-based phenotypic modification may also allow an organism to change its relation to the CNC-inducing environmental factor(s) (e.g., flagella propelled swimming allowing a cell to relocate to a dry surface). This locational change is a straightforward case of RNC, the coming about of which is not only causally enabled by the phenotypic change brought on by an initial instance of CNC but is also a response to the cost of that phenotypic change (e.g., having zero fecundity as a biflagellate). Actively engaging in RNC may, in turn, result in a subsequent instance of CNC occurring (e.g., reversion to a myxamoeba), both jointly restoring the organism's causal relation to environmental factors in a way that has potential fitness effects.

The microcyst stage, I would like to suggest, represents an instance of CNC. Recall that the microcyst is a reversible and optional dormant stage that may interrupt the ameboflagellate stage, provided that the cell encounters unfavourable environmental conditions. For example, when a myxamoeba fails to encounter nutrient resources for an extended period of time or when its immediate environment becomes too dry for long periods of time, these conditions induce the encysting of the cell. Encysting consists of the formation of a resistant cell wall around the ameboflagellate that protects it from potentially harmful environmental factors, allowing it to enter a non-vegetative stage in which energy is radically conserved (Stephenson and Stempen, 1994). Microcyst formation allows the ameboflagellate to maintain its viability in a dormant state until favourable environmental factors are detected and the cell can resume its vegetative existence. Like the transformation from myxamoeba to biflagellate, becoming a microcyst trades fecundity for viability as long as dormancy is maintained. Importantly, exiting the dormant microcyst stage is highly responsive to changes in environmental conditions (Clark and Haskins, 2015). The mechanisms underwriting the conjunction of encysting and excysting can be viewed as determining the selective environment that will be experienced by the ameboflagellate: if conditions are good, revive so as to affect and be affected by those conditions; if conditions remain bad, remain dormant and beyond the reach of those bad conditions. The reversible transformation into a microcyst may thus be viewed as a radical yet temporary modification of organismal features that change the cell's relation to environmental factors. Given Aaby and Ramsey's characterisation of CNC, entering and exiting the microcyst stage exemplifies an instance of CNC.

The microcysts stage is also an optional manner that an ameboflagellate can change its spatio-temporal relation to other colony members and, hence, a revealing case of RNC. One way for an organism to change its spatio-temporal relation with other organisms is to move towards or away from those organisms; another way is for an organism to remain fixed while other organisms spread out. This latter kind of relational change is particularly relevant for myxamoebae, which find themselves in an overcrowded colony. If all myxamoeba cells in a colony do not encyst (but a fair number do) due to overcrowding, then a locationally fixed encysting cell may experience reduced resource competition at a later time (i.e., exiting dormancy to fewer cohabitant cells). Moreover, by interrupting their ameboflagellate vegetative stage, encysting cells immediately reduce competition for those cells in the colony that do not encyst. Thus, I would like to suggest that entering and exiting the microcyst stage can be construed as an instance of RNC mediated by CNC.[10]

The plasmodium's production and use of extracellular slime that is characteristic of this stage represents a paradigmatic example of ENC. To see how, recall that a motile, foraging plasmodium leaves behind an extracellular slime (mucopolysaccharide) trail wherever it migrates. Slime trails are often (but not always) avoided by plasmodia (Reid et al., 2013). Not unlike Hansel and Gretel's breadcrumbs trails, the scattering and following of which allowed them to find their way out of the forest, extracellular slime trails may sometimes be used by a plasmodium as a cue for avoiding previously foraged locations (Smith-Ferguson et al., 2017). This allows a plasmodium to both avoid spending its metabolic resources on (re)visiting areas that are not likely to contain food and, as a result, reach patches containing food faster than it would without the aid of extracellular slime (Reid et al., 2012) (see Section 5). This two-way causal interaction between a plasmodium and its extracellular slime (or the slime trails of other plasmodia) exemplifies how changes made to the physical environment (i.e., extracellular slime trails) can act as feedback so as to constrain a plasmodium's foraging behaviour and thereby change the selection pressures impacting it and/or its conspecifics. A plasmodium's interaction with its extracellular slime reduces the amount of time and energy spent on foraging in complex environments, something which may have direct fitness effects. Given that the inability to detect and follow slime trails has negative fitness effects, we might expect (a) any individuals in the population that fail to be able

---

[10] If the timing of encysting and excysting is influenced by genetic variation, and either encysting or excysting too early or too late can have negative fitness effects, then selection for those variations on timing mechanisms that are tuned to the onset and termination of unfavourable environmental conditions may occur. As such, variation in timing mechanisms underwriting when CNC-mediated RNC occurs can have effects on subsequent evolution.

to exercise this capacity would be outcompeted and (b) that any heritable genetic variations that would allow Physarum to exercise this capacity would be maintained in the population.

The production and use of extracellular slime may also provide a possible example of how ENC and RNC occur in tandem. Whether a plasmodium avoids slime trails will be dependent upon things like the presence and quality of food that can be reached by migrating across extracellular slime (Reid et al., 2013) and/or the nature of biochemical cues reflecting the stressed or well-nourished condition of the plasmodium that left the slime trail (Briard et al., 2020). If a well-nourished plasmodium leaves behind a carbohydrate-rich slime trail and such trails provide nutrients for the growth of red yeast, then a well-nourished plasmodium may also eventually revisit its own slime trail to consume the red yeast that have since grown there (Epstein et al., 2021). This plasmodial fungal farming – if it is indeed a robust phenomenon – seems to be both an instance of ENC and RNC;[11] it is both an active modification of environmental factors (i.e., leaving slime trails) that impact selection pressures (i.e., the availability of food) *because* it influences the spatio-temporal relation between the slime-secreting plasmodium and the growing red yeast. In other words, ENC has the fitness effects that it does because it brings about RNC. The fact that a plasmodium will choose to consume higher quality food over lower quality food (Latty and Beekman, 2010) when there is an option may thus allow it to modify its physical environment with extracellular slime trails in a way that, over time, systematic-ally alters its relationship to the fungi which it consumes; a well-nourished plasmodium brings yeast to it (locally), rather than having to relocate to yeast elsewhere.

When a plasmodium migrates from a food-depleted to a food-abundant site in the same habitat, such migration depends upon its ability to plastically modify its features. During the plasmodial stage, a Physarum is able to change its shape by altering its internal tubular network structure in a matter of hours in response to changes in external conditions (Nakagaki et al., 2004). This structural reconfig-uration that alters the way plasmodia experience their heterogeneous resource environment *as more homogeneous* is analogous to how plants modify their root structure according to changing soil nutrient patch availability (one exception being that plants are sessile and operating at a much slower timescale than plasmodia). And like such plant root reconfiguration may be viewed as an

---

[11] I make this qualification because the oscillatory successional dynamics that Epstein et al. (2021) discovered were based upon an analysis of only five Petri dish 'ecosystems', each of which differed in experimental light exposure conditions. To show that plasmodial yeast farming is a robust phenomenon, this experiment requires replication using many more samples of each ecosystem condition.

instance of CNC, so may the structural modification of a plasmodium in response to fluctuation in food availability.

The fact that plasmodial structural reconfiguration in response to resource fluctuation may be viewed as an instance of CNC has an interesting upshot for understanding the phenomenon of yeast farming: such farming may be viewed as a dynamic process involving organismal *feature modification* (i.e., tubular network restructuring), environmental *factor modification* (i.e., secreting slime trails), and *modification of spatio-temporal relations* between the focal organism and another organism (i.e., changing the relation between slime-secreting plasmodium and growing red yeast). Hence, a more complete (but most likely nonexhaustive) analysis of Physarum yeast farming from the perspective of niche construction might be the following: CNC brings about ENC, which results in RNC, and RNC in turn brings about CNC, resulting in ENC, and so on. This continuous cycle of factor–feature codetermination is maintained as long as the successional dynamics between a plasmodium and yeast colonies are.

What of the sclerotium stage? Might it too exemplify a form of niche construction? Recall that the sclerotium is an optional and reversible dormant stage which is elicited by encountering unfavourable vegetative conditions. Entering this stage involves a dramatic plasmodial cellular modification that includes the encrustation of the protoplasm in addition to various cytological changes allowing for stored energy reserves to be used (Gorman and Wilkins, 1980). Both entering and exiting the sclerotium stage, similar to entering and exiting the microcyst stage, may be viewed as instances of CNC. In transforming into a sclerotium and thus enabling a plasmodium to use stored metabolic resources, a resource-poor environment for a plasmodium becomes a resource-indifferent environment for a sclerotised cell; starvation or drought becomes less relevant to viability maintenance whilst in this stage. Here again, we find a temporary fitness trade-off between fecundity and viability; as long as the plasmodium remains dormant as a sclerotium, it cannot reproduce (i.e., sporulate) but it can remain viable for up to years in conditions that would be deleterious for the non-resistant vegetative plasmodial cell. The sclerotium, in reverting back to a plasmodium under favourable environmental conditions, both regains the ability to commit to sporulation and also becomes once again constrained by the metabolic needs of a vegetative cell.

Lastly, by migrating into the light, a mature and starving plasmodium initiates the process of differentiation, whereby its protoplasm (and protoplasmic contents) becomes distinct fruiting body parts (i.e., the base, the stalk, the spore case, the spores). This process, in turn, culminates in cessation of the vegetative plasmodium and genesis of the multiple reproductive units: haploid spores. Can this transformation from a plasmodium into fruiting bodies be plausibly viewed as a kind of niche construction? Although not as straightforward as the previous examples, this transformation may represent an interesting case of ENC via organismal feature modification, albeit a feature modification that does not qualify as CNC. That the fruiting body stage is irreversible suggests that it is not a means for an individual plasmodium to buffer itself against unfavourable environmental conditions; rather, it is a necessary step along the way to reproduction. This transformation does not change the causal relation of the plasmodium *qua* fruiting body to selection pressures because transforming into a fruiting body coincides with the termination of the plasmodium. Thus, although the transformation into a fruiting body is a radical modification of the plasmodium's features, it fails to be an instance of CNC.

Fruiting bodies are differentiated physical structures *made by* and *from* the plasmodium in support of the development and dispersal of spores (Keller et al., 2008). As such, spore number may be viewed as a (potential) measure of a plasmodium's fecundity, and maturing fruiting bodies are a change made to the physical environment by the pre-fruiting plasmodium in *realising* its fecundity. Fruiting body formation thus may be viewed as a kind of ENC, one that affects how the next generation of ameboflagellates experience their environment by affecting mature spore dispersal. For instance, in comparison to fruiting bodies with shorter stalks, those plasmodia that produce fruiting bodies with taller stalks may be more effective at both protecting the encased spores from excessive moisture and contributing to the dissemination of the dry spore mass because spores are elevated higher above the substratum (Keller et al., 2008). Insofar as such fruiting body character variation (i.e., having taller or shorter stalks) is determined by the genome (and possibly heritable epigenome) of the pre-fruiting plasmodium, such variation is subject to natural selection. A plasmodium's fruiting so as to lift its spores higher off the substrate and indirectly affect spore dispersal is a form of (canalised) ENC-mediated RNC. External niche construction in one generation of entity (the plasmodium), rather than having effects upon the selection pressures which it faces, impacts which selective environment is faced by a subsequent generation of entities with a distinct organisational form (ameboflagellates).

The fruiting body stage, hence, illustrates how ENC-mediated RNC may have effects upon the next generation without such effects being mediated by ecological inheritance. Like a bird's nest, the fruiting body surrounding the spores is a fleeting structure. It is neither used, maintained, nor cumulatively built upon by ameboflagellates or the following generation of plasmodial cells. The characteristics of the mature fruiting body which make it the environmental factor that it is nonetheless affect *which* subsequent factors of the selective environment that ameboflagellates experience.

Taking stock: I have illustrated how some of the stages that *P. polycephalum* completes over the course of its complex life cycle exemplify at least one of the three kinds of niche construction included in Aaby and Ramsey's (2022) tripartite niche construction taxonomy. Moreover, I have shown how some of these stages and the transitions between them reveal different ways that ENC, RNC, and CNC causally interact and occur in tandem. Lastly, I have shown how some of the (reversible and non-reversible) transitions between Physarum's life cycle stages associated with CNC and ENC can be viewed in terms of fitness trade-offs (see Table 2). I will now offer a few considerations regarding the value of looking at complex life cycles for niche construction approaches.

2.6 The Value of Looking at Complex Life Cycles for Niche Construction

What does examining various kinds of niche construction in the context of complex life cycles tell us that looking at them outside such a context cannot? One immediate answer to this question is that complex life cycles provide a broader context in which to explore how different kinds of niche construction interact in a dynamic manner. For example, relation between kinds of niche construction, patterns amongst those relations, and where those patterns arise in one organism's complex life cycle can be used to probe for the presence of such relations and patterns in other taxa. Doing so, would allow niche construction practitioners to confirm either the generalisable nature of such patterns or investigate how such patterns differ due to differences in ecological and life history characteristics (e.g., differences in habitat/microhabitat, trophic relations, reproductive modes and schedules, number of generations within a life cycle, growth rate, dormancy patterns, etc.). Importantly, some of these generalisable patterns may be particular to complex life cycles.

Assuming that looking at niche construction by way of simple life cycles can often reveal complex relations that investigating an individual instance of niche construction in isolation cannot, complex life cycles may potentially offer an *even richer* source of niche construction-relevant phenomena and relations amongst them to investigate. This is due to their being multigenerational and featuring more than one reproductive and/or nuclear phase. For example, although CNC-mediated RNC or RNC-mediated CNC may be relations that are also found in some simple life cycles, the question as to how CNC-mediated RNC and RNC-mediated CNC are sequentially organised within the same life cycle is something that is much more amenable to investigation using complex life cycles. This is because life cycles featuring alternation of generations are more likely to be those that feature both kinds of relation and thus identifying

Table 2 Life cycle stages of *P. polycephalum* (excluding the spore stage), some of the kinds of niche construction arising within and/or between them, and the resulting fitness trade-offs. If there are relations between kinds of niche construction exhibited in the sclerotium stage and/or whether there are fitness trade-offs in the plasmodium stage have not been addressed in the analysis above and remain open questions for future research

Life cycle stages	Types of niche construction	Relations between niche construction types	Fitness trade-offs
Ameboflagellate	**Constitutive**: interconvertible transformation from and to myxamoeba and biflagellate in response to the presence or absence of free water	**Relational mediated constitutive niche construction**: relational niche construction as a means of bringing about subsequent constitutive niche construction.	Temporarily suspending fecundity to maintain viability (as biflagellate)
	Relational: a biflagellate's swimming to a dry substrate from a water microhabitat, resuming the ability to asexually reproduce as a myxamoeba		
Microcyst	**Constitutive**: optional and reversible transformation from ameboflagellate to resistant, dormant unit in response to drought, abundance of metabolic by-products, overabundance of cells, and/or starvation	**Constitutive mediated relational niche construction**: constitutive niche construction as a means of bringing about subsequent relational niche construction.	Temporarily suspending fecundity to maintain viability
	Relational: encysting that alters the spatio-temporal relation of the ameboflagellate to other cells in the colony, possibly reducing resource competition		

Table 2 (cont.)

Life cycle stages	Types of niche construction	Relations between niche construction types	Fitness trade-offs
Plasmodium	**External**: depositing and using extracellular slime for improved navigation and efficient foraging in complex environments **Relational**: allowing red yeast to grow on deposited carbohydrate-rich extracellular slime for later consumption **Constitutive**: structural reconfiguration of the internal network of tubes in response to resource fluctuation	**Cyclical niche construction:** constitutive niche construction brings about external niche construction, which results in relational niche construction that in turn brings about further constitutive niche construction and more of the same	?
Sclerotium	**Constitutive**: optional and reversible transformation from plasmodium to resistant, dormant unit in response to drought, light, and/or starvation	?	Temporarily suspending fecundity to maintain viability
Fruiting Body	**External**: plasmodial transformation into partially non-living environmental structures that support the development and dispersal of spores	**External mediated relational niche construction:** external niche construction as a means of bringing about relational niche construction in next generation	Permanently suspending viability for fitness of next generation

patterns between those relations becomes possible in such a context. To stress, I am not suggesting that investigating niche construction should proceed by exclusively investigating complex life cycles. To the contrary, I am suggesting a pluralist approach that urges a supplementary use of complex life cycles to buttress and fill out investigations of niche construction that have focused exclusively upon individual instances of feature–factor modification outside of the broader context of (simple or complex) life cycles.

In this section, I have used Physarum's life cycle to exemplify how complex multigenerational life cycles, despite being biological phenomena that may at first glance seem unrelated to niche construction, can be used as a valuable manner of investigating niche construction. In Section 3, we shall take a closer look at Physarum's spores, considering a puzzle that is to do with the fact that dormant spores lack one of the features that many biologists agree is characteristic of life on Earth – metabolism – and are yet considered an example of life.

3 On the Biotic Status of Spores

There have been numerous theories of life proposed by different biologists and philosophers, many of which have been partially (if not wholly) motivated by a desire to understand the origins of life on Earth, the possible forms of life beyond Earth, and/or the relationship between life and cognition (Cleland, 2019). When one asks, 'what is life?', one common way of going about investigating this question is to ask, 'what makes some entity a living system?' – that entity being any acknowledged example of life. Answering the latter question is supposed to shed light on the former – the former presupposing some agreement about examples of life and asking what properties those examples have in common. Let's call the general view that questions about life are questions about living (and vice versa) 'life-living equivalence'. Some prominent theories, assuming life-living equivalence, have looked to reproduction and active metabolic exchange processes as necessary but non-sufficient conditions for being a living system and, hence, being necessary for life as we know it. While non-reproducing, yet unarguably living, mules present at least one counterexample to the notion that reproduction is necessary for life, in this section, I will focus exclusively upon metabolic exchange and how attention to the biotic status of dormant spores (i.e., whether they qualify as living, dead, or as some other living-related state) might bring some clarity to the concept of life.

Since dormant spores neither take in energy resources from their environment nor output waste, they are metabolically inert entities. Despite being metabolically inert, spores are recognised by biologists as an example of life.

Such explicit recognition is clear, for instance, on NASA's Office of Safety & Mission Assurance (OSMS) webpage, where they write on bacterial spores:

> 'Spores are the most likely form of terrestrial life to be able to survive on another planet' https://sma.nasa.gov/sma-disciplines/planetary-protection/ explore/explore-item/what-are-spores.

That biologists also view spores as exemplifying life is evidenced by the fact that they are regarded as stages in life cycles of spore-forming organisms (Section 2.2). It would be truly odd if spores were considered devoid of life and yet featured as a developmental stage within a life cycle.

The claims that dormant spores are an example of life *and* that a living system must necessarily engage in metabolic processes, however, pull in different directions when assuming life-living equivalence. For if spores are an example of life, then, deploying life-living equivalence, they are also living systems. However, in taking the assumption onboard that metabolic activity is necessary for life, spores also turn out to be non-living systems because they do not engage in metabolic activity. Taken together, we arrive at the conclusion that dormant spores are both living systems and non-living systems. Two ways of avoiding this *reductio ad absurdum* that make sense of the fact that biologists regard dormant spores as an example of life are to: (1) maintain life-living equivalence and relax the condition that metabolic exchange is necessary for being a living system *or* (2) keep the condition that metabolic exchange is necessary for being a living system and abandon life-living equivalence.

In this section, I will build a case for the second option, arguing that the relevant equivalence is between life and being alive (rather than life and living), and that living is a way of being alive. To illustrate and develop this position I will articulate a taxonomical analysis of the biotic status of Physarum spores – an analysis that can be generalised to other spore-forming taxa given the shared biotic features of spores. This section will have the following organisation: firstly, I will survey some examples of metabolic definitions of life that have been introduced in biology (and biology-related fields), highlighting how these definitions deploy life-living equivalence and, hence, assume that engaging in metabolic exchange is not only necessary for being a living system but also necessary for life. Turning to Physarum spores, I will briefly look at their metabolic inert (dormant) state and then articulate one reason why biologists consider ametabolic dormant spores an example of life. Nick Lane's (2016) distinction between 'living' and 'being alive' will then be elucidated and used as the basis for taxonomising the biotic status of Physarum's spores (and spores of other taxa) in support of option (2). Lastly, I will deploy the proposed taxonomy to consider spore ageing and its relation to senescence in vegetative entities, illustrating one of the wider implications of this taxonomy.

3.1 Is Metabolism a Requirement for Life?

Amongst the various ways that life has been conceptualised, the idea that metabolism is a necessary component of life has been central to many of them. Spelling this out has usually, but not always, taken the form of *defining* life in terms of metabolism, where such definitions are based upon the examples of life that we have observed on Earth. Setting aside the obvious problem of basing a definition of universal life (i.e., life on Earth and beyond) upon a sample of one (i.e., earthly life) (Cleland, 2018), in what follows I shall only be interested in what can be said about life as we know it – on Earth. Whether there is reason to believe that life on Earth is representative of life everywhere will not be taken up here. Some of the metabolic definitions and characterisations of life that have been previously suggested will be used as a jumping-off point to illustrate that many biologists view metabolism as a necessary condition for life and that questions about life are often equated with questions about living (i.e., life-living equivalence).

So, what is metabolism? Metabolism may be characterised as the sum of all biochemical processes by which a system extracts energy from its environment, uses that energy in a controlled fashion to maintain its organisation despite the material turnover of its component parts, and produces metabolic waste. Metabolism is typically understood as consisting of two processes: 'catabolism' and 'anabolism'. Catabolism is the breaking down of energy resources (e.g., carbohydrates from food), releasing energy contained in chemical bonds. Anabolism is the use of that released energy for cellular function, growth, and repair via the synthesis of proteins, nucleic acids, and adenosine triphosphate (ATP).[12] As such, catabolism and anabolism can be viewed as converse and yet coupled reactions, the former *producing energy* for use and the latter *using energy* for further energy production. Metabolism also involves making waste products. Metabolic waste is any surplus and/or toxic by-product of metabolic reactions that cannot be used for the maintenance of cellular function. These products take the form of solid, liquid, gaseous, and heat products, and are returned to the environment in ways that are often powered by metabolism. I will use 'metabolic exchange' as shorthand to refer to the combination of all of these processes.

How might metabolic exchange feature into a definition of life? Carl Sagan, providing an overview (and also a stinging critique) of various definitions of life in his now-classic *Encyclopaedia Britannica* entry 'Definitions of Life', describes a standard metabolic definition of life as one based upon the idea that

---

[12] ATP is an energy-supplying molecule that is often referred to as the cellular 'energy currency' because its breakdown via catabolism supplies a source of energy that is used for the vast majority of cellular functions.

> a living system is an object with a definite boundary, continually exchanging
> some of its materials with its surroundings, but without altering its general
> properties at least over some period of time. (Sagan, [1970] 2010: 303)

A living system, according to this definition, is one that is delimited by
a boundary (e.g., a membrane, cell wall, etc.) and that continuously engages
in metabolic exchange with its environment. Although a boundary is not an
explicit feature of metabolic exchange, it is something that many metabolic
definitions of life feature. One reason for this is that boundaries provide a way of
controlling what happens on the inside of that boundary – not everything gets in
or out. Similarly, the idea that a system exchanges energy and waste with its
environment is premised upon it – the system – having a boundary that separates
it from its environment. Sagan's definition also highlights the idea that a living
system's general properties remain unaltered (at least for a while) despite the
ongoing metabolic exchange that occurs.

Autopoetic theory offers another example of how metabolism is considered to
be a defining feature of living systems. Autopoetic definitions are admittedly
abstract, tending to focus upon the organisational logic of circular 'self-
production' (Maturana and Varela, 1980). This is the idea that metabolic processes, and hence living processes, are those that circularly produce the system's
organisation and are produced by the system's organisation. This kind of recur-
sive self-production, according to autopoietic theory, is responsible for the self-
sustaining property that is particular to living systems; it explains their autonomy,
something that distinguishes them from inanimate or dead systems. Interpreting
Maturana and Varela (1973), philosopher Michael Bitbol and biochemist Pier
Luigi Luisi provide the following autopoietic definition of life:

> [L]ife is a cyclic process that produces the components that in turn self-
> organise in the process itself, and all within a boundary of its own making.
> (Bitbol and Luigi, 2004: 99).

Yet, another example of how metabolic exchange is viewed as an essential
component of life is provided by the Hungarian biologist Tibor Gánti ([1970]
2003). In the context of his Chemoton theory of minimal life, Gánti offers a list
of necessary conditions for life, what he calls 'real (absolute) life criteria'.
Contending that a 'living system has to perform metabolism' (104), Gánti
unpacks this necessary criterion for life as follows:

> By metabolism we understand the active or passive entrance of material and
> energy into the system which transforms them by chemical processes into its
> own internal constituents. Waste products are also produced, so that the chemical
> reactions result in a regulated and controlled increase of the inner constituents as
> well as in the energy supply of the system. (Gánti, [1970] 2003: 76)

Similar to Sagan's standard metabolic definition, Gánti's necessary (but not sufficient) criterion emphasises the extraction of energy from the environment into a bounded system that is then broken down (i.e., catabolism) and used to construct the system's component parts (i.e., anabolism) in a controlled and regulated manner. And like Sagan's standard definition, Gánti's criterion is explicit about the nature of the products of metabolic exchange (i.e., internal constituents and waste products). Gánti's criterion is, however, more akin to the autopoetic definition of life in the sense that it emphasises the circular self-production of the metabolising system. Interestingly, of all three accounts, Gánti's criterion is the only one which mentions the production of waste.

These three examples are representative of a more general and long-standing view in biology that metabolic exchange is necessary for life.[13] Moreover, I would like to argue that these examples suggest that *at least some* biologists assume life-living equivalence and the fact that at least some biologists assume life-living equivalence is enough to motivate the development of the biotic taxonomy that will follow (Section 3.3). How might this be the case? Take for example Sagan's description of a metabolic definition. That which is being defined is life. This is evident given the title of the encyclopaedia entry is 'Definitions of Life'. Sagan, however, then goes on to define *what a living system is*. This switch from life to living is only justified against a background of life-living equivalence. For answering the question 'what is a living system?' is supposed to shed light on what life is.[14]

What about Bitbol and Luisi? At first blush, their interpretation of Maturana and Varela seems innocent enough. Upon closer inspection, however, their use of life-living equivalence surfaces. Bitbol and Luisi offer a definition of life, as is evidenced by their writing 'life is', and then provide a metabolic definition. So far, so good. However, Maturana and Varela's autopoietic theory is focused upon defining *living systems*. This is clear when they write:

> [W]e shall first characterise the kind of machines that living systems are and then show how peculiar properties of living systems may arise as a consequence of the organisation of this kind of machines [sic]. (1973: 78)

and then:

> An autopoietic machine is a machine organised (defined as a unity) as a network of processes of production (transformation and destruction) of

---

[13] The idea that life requires metabolism (and reproduction) goes at least as far back as Aristotle, who is often considered the father of biology.

[14] Although Sagan was an astronomer, not a biologist, I think it's fair to say that his deployment of life-living equivalence is representative of a general attitude adopted by many of the biologists that he attributes his standard metabolic definition to.

components which: (i) through their interactions and transformations continuously regenerate and realise the network of processes (relations) that produced them; and (ii) constitute it (the machine) as a concrete unity in space in which they (the components) exist by specifying the topological domain of its realization as such a network. (Maturana and Varela, 1973: 78–79)

Maturana and Varela are careful to focus upon living systems as their intended objects of analysis and do not, as Bitbol and Luisi's interpretation suggests, equate definitions of living systems with definitions of life.[15] Bitbol and Luisi's interpretation of Maturana and Varela's autopoietic definition of living system exemplifies life-living equivalence and how readily it is assumed even by the likes of careful biologists and philosophers.

Gánti's definition also assumes life-living equivalence. His real- (absolute) life criteria turn out to be necessary and sufficient conditions for being a living system. Metabolic exchange, a real- (absolute) life criterion, is something that livings systems must perform.

If these examples are representative of a general acceptance and use of life-living equivalence on the part of biologists and philosophers, then a problem arises in the context of understanding the biotic status of dormant spores.[16] For anyone who assumes life-living equivalence takes metabolic exchange as necessary for being living system is committed to an incoherent view if there are metabolically inert examples of life.[17] Dormant spores, as we have already seen, are one such example that most biologists acknowledge as such. Let us now turn to look at Physarum spores in particular, focusing on what makes spores metabolically inert and why one might plausibly consider them to be an example of life. Although Physarum spores differ in some respects from those of bacteria, something that I will soon clarify in more detail, there are shared physiological changes that underly spore dormancy across taxa. It is the

---

[15] Interestingly, later in an article entitled On Defining Life, Varela (1994) presents a similar definition for (minimal) living systems. Given his earlier work (1973) with Maturana, his use of life-living equivalence comes as a surprise to me.

[16] Let it be stressed that the use of life-living equivalence is by no means limited to the context of metabolic definitions (or theories) of life. Its prevalence extends to all aspects of biological theorising that looks to expound upon life and biotic processes (e.g., theories and definitions of life based upon reproduction, thermodynamics, etc.). The argument that I present here is merely one manner to motivate renouncing life-living equivalence. A more general motivation, as I hope to show, comes from the potential usefulness and conceptual clarity of the biotic taxonomy that I develop in Section 3.3.

[17] This is not meant to suggest that any of those authors who are committed to metabolic definitions expounded upon above do or do not acknowledge that there are metabolically inert systems that are examples of life. I am merely stating that if any of them do acknowledge that there are metabolically inert systems that are examples of life, then given their use of life-living equivalence their position is incoherent.

presence of these commonalities which allow using an investigation into Physarum spores as a manner of understanding the biotic status of spores as they are found across all taxa.

3.2 Putting Metabolism on Temporary Hold

In order to understand the metabolically inert nature of dormant spores in Physarum, it is necessary to understand the process of spore development. Recall that during the process of sporulation, a starved plasmodial cell differentiates into multiple fruiting bodies (Section 2.3). Within the apical end of each fruiting body the cellular cytoplasm cleaves, after which meiotic recombination leads to the development of mononucleate haploid spores. Spore cellularisation is completed as a thick, resistant cell wall develops around each compartmentalised nucleus and its surrounding cytoplasm, forming individual spores within the spore case. As they mature over the hours that follow, spores (and the spore cases that surround them) undergo a process of desiccation. Such drying out enables spores to be light enough to be easily dispersed by wind, and seeing as they are reproductive units (cells), wide dispersal increases the progeny's (ameboflagellates) chance of survival by decreasing resource competition. Desiccation is due to the spore cases being vertically suspended on stalks, and thus, being distanced from the moist substrate and exposed to air flow. As each spore dries out, it loses the majority of its water content and metabolism ceases.

Why does cell desiccation result in its metabolism coming to a grinding halt? The answer, put in simple terms, is this: metabolism involves various chemical reactions that can only occur within a medium of water (Wharton, 2003). So, when cellular water is depleted to 20 per cent or below of its normal content, it is inferred that metabolism has ceased (Clegg, 1979). It is under these physiological conditions that a spore becomes dormant and thus metabolically inert.

This brings us to the next crucial question. Despite their being ametabolic, why might desiccated spores be considered examples of life? A hint is provided by Gánti, who describing the state of ametabolic entities writes:

> A system suitable for the occurrence of the processes in question may be either functioning or in a state which is not functioning but is capable of doing so. When this system is in its functioning state it is said to be living; when it is in its non-functioning but functionable state it is capable of living, but it is not dead. ([1970] 2003: 75)

I believe one implicit reason why many biologists acknowledge dormant spores to be forms of life – a reason made explicit here by Gánti – has to do with the idea that they *retain a capacity to engage in metabolic exchange*. Let me take a moment to unpack this idea and put some 'biological meat' on what might seem at first to be an abstract concept.

Were most organisms to undergo desiccation, they would die in the process; their cellular structure would be destroyed beyond repair due to protein denaturation (i.e., altering the shape or conformity of the proteins and hence preventing them from playing a role in the various metabolic and regulatory functions that they typically underwrite). This is not the case, however, with spores. In fact, desiccation allows spores to remain viable despite the cessation of metabolism that desiccation brings about, a process generally referred to as 'anhydrobiosis'.[18] During anhydrobiosis in eukaryotic spores, it is thought that most cellular water is replaced by a sugar ('trehalose') that protects the structure of proteins and membranes from the destructive effects of water loss (Clegg, 2001; Rikkinen et al., 2019).[19]

In an anhydrobiotic state, if all goes well, a spore retains its capacity to engage in metabolic exchange despite being metabolically inert. If something goes awry and the spore loses this capacity, it dies and hence fails to be an example of life any longer. I think this is an important point. If we don't recognise a spore as alive, then we can't make sense of the significance of its structure being destroyed. We wouldn't be able to see this as 'death', but just an ordinary physical degradation.

Suppose a desiccated spore encounters environmental water (or a moist surface) again, and the preserved intercellular structure and membrane are put to work once more so that metabolic exchange resumes. When this happens, a spore's capacity to engage in metabolic exchange is *utilised*. To be sure, even when not utilising its capacity to metabolise, a spore retains that capacity (much in the same way that your capacity to breathe does not somehow vanish when you begin to breathe again after having held your breath for some seconds). Retaining the capacity (unutilised or utilised) to engage in metabolic exchange qualifies spores as examples of life and the mechanism underwriting anhydrobiosis describes *how* a dormant spore retains its capacity to metabolise despite its being unutilised. The continued functioning of metabolic pathways, on the other hand, is how a non-dormant spore retains its capacity for metabolising; the capacity is retained by utilising that very capacity. Non-dead dogs, bees,

---

[18] Although the term 'anhydrobiosis' was not coined until 1959 by Keilin, that an organism's metabolism could come to a reversible halt was discovered around 300 years earlier by Antony van Leeuwenhoek whilst doing experiments with desiccated 'animacules' (rotifers) that he obtained from his gutter. Other anhydrobiotic organisms include tardigrades, brine shrimp, some nematodes, resurrection plants, and some bacteria.

[19] The idea that water is replaced by trehalose during anhydrobiosis is known as the 'water replacement hypothesis' and was proposed by James Clegg (1986).

evergreens, octopuses, humans, and bacteria, all undoubtable examples of life in biology, share this capacity to engage in metabolic exchange.[20]

Zooming out for a moment: anhydrobiosis in Physarum is coupled to reproduction, and because of this, what survives when metabolism resumes (when the spore utilises its capacity to engage in metabolic exchange after dormancy) is not the plasmodium that sporulated. Again, the plasmodium (and the generation that it represents) terminates with the nuclear cellularisation of the fruiting body. Instead, it a plasmodium's progeny that survives via the spore stage of the life cycle (Section 2.4). This may be contrasted to bacterial spores. In the case of bacteria, the same organisational form that transforms into a spore hatches from the spore after germination; the bacterium that emerges after germination is a continuation of the bacterial cell generation that sporulated. In this sense, bacterial spores are more akin to Physarum sclerotia and microcysts, all of which represent reversible (and optional) dormant stages within their different life cycles.

There may be an interesting sense, however, in which one can view *spore development* in terms of a reversible transformation. This requires zooming in again. A transformation from (1) a metabolising spore directly after nuclear cellularisation to (2) a metabolically inert spore in an anhydrobiotic state and then back again to a (3) metabolically active spore during germination.[21] The reason that I have suggested why spores are acknowledged as examples of life turns upon this fine-grained picture. The capacity to engage in metabolic exchange remains constant throughout this transformation although that capacity is only utilised in steps (1) and (3). It is in this sense that one might say that the spore stage represents an irreversible transition *in the life cycle* of an acellular slime mould, and it also represents a reversible metabolic transition *in spore development*. Being able to separate these fine-grained (i.e., spore development) and coarse-grained (i.e., Physarum's life cycle) views is important because they provide two different informative perspectives to consider and compare when analysing spores. Remaining aware of these two different perspectives when focusing upon Physarum should make this quite apparent.

Having articulated one shared quality of life – one that I suspect lies at the heart of at least some biologists' intuitions that dormant spores qualify as life – I would now like to put it to use in formulating a way of resolving the tension that was articulated in Section 3. Recall that this tension arises when one,

---

[20] Any of these organisms when dead, rather than representing an example of life, represent an example of a biomarker – a sign of life that once existed.

[21] See Segev et al. (2012) for evidence that entry into dormancy lasts several days for bacteria *B. subtilis*. This spore development period in *B. subtilis* would be analogous to what I have labelled period (1) in the development of Physarum spores.

assuming life-living equivalence, holds onto the idea that metabolic exchange is necessary for being a living system and yet acknowledges that biologists regard spores as an example of life. The way of resolving this tension that I will now pursue involves jettisoning life-living equivalence and developing a taxonomy around a distinction proposed by Lane (2016).

3.3 Being Alive versus Living

Molecular biologist Nick Lane, in his book *The Vital Question*, examines why eukaryotes and the kind of traits that are characteristic to them (i.e., nuclei, organelles, sex, and phagocytosis) have only evolved once from a single prokaryotic predecessor in the four billon years that prokaryotes have existed on Earth. In approaching this question, Lane asks a more fundamental one: what is living? He considers what metabolically inert entities such as dormant spores can suggest about life given that they are 'completely stable in their non-living state' (2016: 55) and in doing so, he writes something rather revealing:

> That [remaining stable in a non-living state] tells us something about the difference between life and living. Spores are not technically living, even though most biologists would classify them as alive, because they retain a potential to revive. They can go back to living so they are not dead. (Lane, 2016: 55; my addition).

Lane, referring to dormant spores, distinguishes between life and living and, as such, does not assume what I have been calling life-living equivalence. He does, however, as I read him, suggest that being alive is necessary and sufficient for life, what might be called 'life-alive equivalence'. Importantly, he suggests that retaining a potential to revive – *to go back to living* – is necessary for being alive. In order to make sense of this condition, we must first have an idea of what living is since being alive is characterised relative to living. In elucidating what he takes to be the difference between life (being alive) and living, Lane writes:

> Life is about structure (dictated in part by genes and evolution) but living – growing and proliferating – is as much about the environment, how structure and environment interrelate. (2016: 55)

Lane's characterisation of the difference between life and living in terms of structure and structure–environment interrelations may be plausibly viewed as providing rough explanations of the two different ways that an entity can retain a capacity to metabolise. More precisely, having the right structure explains how the capacity to engage in metabolic change is retained without utilising it. On the other hand, having the right structure *and* that structure's having the right ongoing interrelation with the environment explains how the capacity to engage in metabolic exchange is both retained *and* utilised. To see this, consider that a dormant spore is alive because its structure has been preserved in an anhydrobiotic state, allowing it to retain its capacity to engage in metabolism; yet a dormant spore fails to be a living entity since that capacity is not being utilised. On the other hand, a germinating spore – one that has encountered favourable environmental conditions – is both alive and living. It utilises its capacity to engage in metabolic exchange, and also retains that capacity in virtue of its structure. This is also true of the pre-dormant spore. Lane's distinction between being alive and living thus lends support to the idea articulated above that dormant spores are acknowledged to be life because they retain the capacity to engage in metabolic exchange. Lane fleshes this idea out with the notion of preserved structure.

Assuming that this analysis is correct, living can be viewed as something that is additional to being alive – it requires more than just having the right structure. To understand how living builds upon being alive and yet both categories remain distinct, consider the fact that being a member of the species *P. polycephalum* is distinct from being a member of the genus *Physarum* (see Table 1). That this is the case is compatible with the fact that being a *P. polycephalum* is *a specific way of being* a *Physarum*. This kind of relation is often described by philosophers in terms of being a 'specification relation', 'where the more specific property can be understood as a conjunction of the less specific property and some independent property or properties' (Wilson, 2023: 1). Living may be viewed as a species of the genus being alive in the same way that *P. polycephalum* is a species of the genus *Physarum*. This has the result that any entity that is living is also alive (having the right structure *and* having the right interrelation with the environment so as to utilise that structure), although there may be entities that are alive which simultaneously fail to be living (only possessing the right structure). It is in this way that living builds upon being alive – it is a way of being alive.

Lane, in the passage above, also describes living in terms of 'growing and proliferating'. Whether he sees growing and proliferation (i.e., reproduction) as contingent features or necessary features of living is not clear. I would like to argue that although vegetative growth and repair – protein synthesis – is part and parcel of utilised metabolism (anabolism) and hence living, there is a reason to view proliferation as a contingent feature of living systems. For example, a metabolising and hence living Physarum spore is not a reproducing entity but a reproductive cell that develops under suitable conditions into a reproducing entity. In this sense, a non-dormant spore is similar to a metabolising sperm cell or egg cell, none of which proliferate. Although non-dormant spores cannot reproduce, protein synthesis occurs until a spore enters dormancy (Sauer et al., 1969) and again during germination. One general take home from this example is that being a living system and being a proliferating system can come apart, although in many cases they do not.

3.4 Dead, *Structura Vivens*, or Living: A Taxonomy

With these conceptual distinctions to hand, I would like to suggest that the biotic status of Physarum spores can fall into one of three possible categories: dead, '*structura vivens*', – which literally translates from Latin into 'living structure' – or, living (henceforth referred to as the 'DSVL taxonomy'). The last two states constitute the domain of life. Dormant spores fall into the category of *structura vivens*; they are entities that are alive and with the right structure for living yet they are not living. Pre-dormant and germinating spores fall in the category of living and hence also alive. Spores that have lost their capacity to engage in metabolic exchange fall into the category of dead (i.e., lifeless) and are thus neither living nor alive (see Figure 3). There are no sharp cut-offs that exist between these categories given that both retaining the capacity to metabolise and utilising a retained capacity to metabolise are dependent on biological processes (e.g., intracellular replacement of water with trehalose) that are graded. Even dying takes time, whether it occurs via ageing or more rapidly

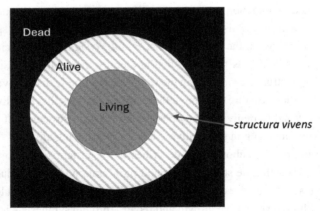

Figure 3 Dead, alive, or living (DAL) taxonomy – conceptual space: life refers to being alive or both being alive and living; living is a way of being alive. Dead excludes any instance of life and as such excludes both being alive and living. Being alive excludes being dead. Any living entity is also alive but some entities that are alive are not living. Although I have represented these categories as being sharp, something that is useful for the sake of explication, I take it that there are no sharp cut-offs that exist between any of these categories.

as a result of injury. Since the biological processes that give rise to the separation of the categories *structura vivens*, living, and dead are not discrete, these categories are themselves rendered fuzzy – exemplifying the kind of fuzzy boundaries that are typical in the biological world.

The focus of this section thus far has largely been two of the three biotic states which I have argued apply to Physarum spores (*structura vivens* and living). A third biotic state, dead, which I have given less attention is, however, no less important. When we think of death, we tend to intuitively think of irreversibly passing from a state of living to one devoid of life altogether. This is an oversimplification of a complex picture that is largely due to the fact that our intuitions are based upon what we know best – human life – and this is not representative of all life.

Different ways of influencing environmental selection effects that have evolved over time, and resulted in stage-specific phenotypes within a life cycle, have also opened up different ways that life can cease to be. Currently, it is thought that in the acellular slime moulds (myxomycetes), the ameboflagellate stage was ancestral to the plasmodial life cycle stage (Collins, 1979). Alone this would suggest not only that sexual reproduction is an evolved trait in the acellular slime moulds but, crucially, that sclerotisation and sporulation (see Section 2) evolved from a life cycle that consisted exclusively of asexually reproducing ameboflagellates. Let this sink in for a minute. The ability to decouple being alive from living evolved at least two separate times in the acellular slime moulds (myxomycetes) with the evolution of the sclerotia and the reproductive spore (and possibly a third with the microcyst). The evolution of these different life cycle stages resulted in not only new ways to meet selection pressures head-on but also new ways to die.

For Physarum, death can occur from not only from a state of living but also from a state being alive. When a Physarum dies from a state of living, it dies from a state of either being an ameboflagellate, a plasmodium, a reviving sclerotium, a young fruiting body, an immature spore, or a germinating spore. When a Physarum dies from a state of *structura vivens*, it dies whilst either being a sclerotium, a microcyst, or a dormant spore. Let us now take a moment to consider *how* a spore might die.

Given that being alive is about preserving structure (Lane, 2016), one way for a spore to die is for it to somehow lose its life-bearing structure and, as a result, irreversibly lose its capacity to engage in metabolic exchange. This degradation may occur across a wide range of rates. At one extreme, a spore can suffer significant structural damage instantaneously to such a degree that the capacity to metabolise is altogether thwarted; at the other extreme it may suffer structural deterioration over time such that the capacity to metabolise becomes increasingly limited and is slowly lost. Both are changes to the structural integrity of the spore. The most vivid examples of the former extreme of structural damage are a spore's being destroyed by being crushed or digested. The latter extreme of structural deterioration is spore ageing, something that is measured by the reduced rate of germination (Smith and Robinson, 1975; Segev et al., 2012).[22] Either significant structural damage or structural deterioration over time and their accompanying DNA damage and/or protein modification may render a spore dead. This covers all three possible categories of the DSVL taxonomy that biotic status of Physarum spores may fall into.

The DSVL taxonomy may be distinguished from the taxonomy elucidated by Clegg (2001) and Wharton (2003), both of whom contend that biological organisation may be classified in terms of three different biotic states: alive, dead, and cryptobiotic. As I understand their taxonomy, 'alive' refers to being metabolically active, whilst 'cryptobiotic' refers the state of metabolic standstill occurring in response to various physical stresses, including desiccation (anhydrobiosis), freezing (cryptobiosis), and osmotic stress (osmobiosis) (Keilin, 1959). However, by conceptualising the difference between being *structura vivens* and living in terms of retaining a capacity to metabolise and utilising that retained capacity, the DSVL taxonomy offers the advantage over Clegg and Wharton's taxonomy of being able to capture the specification relation between being alive and living. As conceptualised by Clegg and Wharton, the notion of 'alive' (metabolically active) cannot coherently *be a specific way of being* cryptobiotic (metabolically inactive). This is undesirable because when answering a question like 'what makes a dormant spore a form a life?' (or equally 'what makes a dormant spore alive?') one of the things that biologists presumably would like to do is identify the shared feature(s) of dormant and non-dormant spores. The DSVL taxonomy, in capturing the specification relation between alive and living captures at least one such feature: dormant and non-dormant spores both retain the capacity to engage in metabolic exchange via their preserved structure. Entering into an anhydrobiotic state is how spore structure is preserved and how ametabolic dormant spores remain alive like non-dormant spores.

3.4.1 Generalising the DSVL Taxonomy

The DSVL taxonomy provides a clear manner for thinking about the biotic status of Physarum spores and those of other spore-producing taxa over the

---

[22] Instantaneous damage suffered by a spore may also not be severe enough for it to result in immediate death; rather, such damage may only be fatal after an organism begins to utilise its capacity to metabolise again. A telling case of this type is provided by Wharton (2003), who describes Hinton's (1960) observation of an anhydrobiotic larva of the midge *P. vanderplanki*. The larva, after suffering damage during its dormancy, revived only to die as a result of that damage.

course of spore development (the zoomed-in perspective). This is because of the common structural and physiological features that are shared by all spores. The DSVL taxonomy can also be used to understand how each stage occurring within a life cycle or when dead is related to others in virtue of their shared biotic status (the zoomed-out perspective).

What is the scientific value of recognising these shared biotic relations? To take an example using stages of Physarum's life cycle: dormant spores are analogous to sclerotia and microcysts in being non-living entities that are nevertheless alive; they are entities with the right structure for living and hence alive and yet they are not living; they are *structura vivens*. Grouping the entities of these respective stages as *structura vivens* prompts us to ask questions about the different underlying mechanisms allowing such entities to remain alive without utilising their capacity to engage in metabolism. The replacement of water with trehalose during anhydrobiosis is one – but most likely not the only – mechanism underwriting the retained capacity of dormant spores to metabolise, but it remains an open question as to whether the same mechanism of water replacement is (at least partly) responsible for how both sclerotia and microcysts remain alive.

Importantly, in recognising these entities as having the same biotic status it is natural to pose questions regarding the differences and/or similarities between their structure preserving mechanisms. If both plasmodia and spore-producing fruiting bodies were evolutionary additions to an ancestral ameboflagellate life cycle (Collins, 1979), then we might expect that the mechanisms underwriting the structural preservation of dormant spores and sclerotia built off of those that allowed microcysts to remain *structura vivens*. That is, early structure preserving mechanisms in dormant microcysts may have laid the ground for further evolutionary innovation, resulting in two additional manners of decoupling being alive from living in the complexifying life cycle of acellular slime moulds. Whether or not this is the case is a question to be scientifically pursued.

To be clear, I am not saying that questions about the mechanisms underlying dormancy cannot be posed or approached without the DSVL Taxonomy. They can and have (Clegg, 2001; Wharton, 2003). Rather, my claim is simply that the conceptual distinctions of the DSVL taxonomy make these kinds of questions easier to formulate and help them to remain contextualised within the larger domain of inquiry – life; a domain that includes both dormant entities and metabolising entities alike.

Another way of generalising the DSVL taxonomy is to use it to compare the biotic status of various life cycle stages of different taxa. Such a comparison prompts interesting questions constrained by the concepts of 'dead', '*structura vivens*', and 'living' and the relations amongst them. For instance, we may compare the biotic status of the stages making up the life cycle of the bacterium *Bacillus subtilis* with those of Physarum. Upon identifying the stages in which *B. subtilis* is *structura vivens* (i.e., dormant), the question of how *B. subtilis* spores preserve their structure and whether those structure preserving mechanisms are similar to those underwriting spores, sclerotia, and/or microcysts in Physarum can be posed (assuming that the mechanisms underwriting structural preservation in the latter three stages differ to some degree). Examples of how the DSVL taxonomy applies to spores across taxa, to each of the organisational forms making up Physarum's complex life cycle, and to organisational forms of *Bacillus* is provided in Figure 4(a–d).

It should be clear that while the conceptual distinctions of the DSVL taxonomy are conducive towards thinking about the biotic status of spores, the uses of the taxonomy are by no means limited to thinking about spores. It can be applied to any organism but will provide the most insightful perspective on those organisms which have evolved a capacity to decouple being alive from

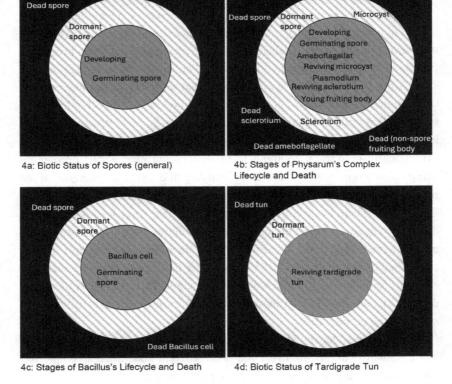

4a: Biotic Status of Spores (general)

4b: Stages of Physarum's Complex Lifecycle and Death

4c: Stages of Bacillus's Lifecycle and Death

4d: Biotic Status of Tardigrade Tun

Figure 4 (a–d)

living. For example, tardigrades do not form dormant spores; however, they can enter into various reversable dormant states and remain alive by balling up and forming a resistant 'tun' during unfavourable conditions (Møbjerg and Cardoso Neves, 2021) (Figure 4d). Although water replacement with trehalose may be a common feature between dormant spores and dormant anhydrobiotic tuns (Wharton, 2003), deploying the DSVL taxonomy prompts us to ask whether the transition back to the state of living for both desiccated spores (i.e., spore germination) and desiccated tuns (i.e., tun reviving) are similar processes. This highlights that there are at least two *explananda* (phenomena to be explained) when it comes to the developmental transitions that take place across the domain of life: how some living entity transitions to being *structura vivens* and how that entity goes back to living again.

3.5 Spore Ageing

When comparing different taxa that have evolved the capacity to decouple being alive from living, one thing that becomes apparent is that some of them can remain alive in an ametabolic state longer than others. One recent finding suggesting a species of nematode has been revived after 46,000 years of anhydrobiotic dormancy in the Siberian permafrost (see Shatilovich et al., 2023).[23] Narrowing the focus once again to spores: dormant bacterial spores have been revived after being trapped in amber for twenty-five to forty million years (Cano and Borucki 1995). Dormant Physarum spores have a considerably shorter period of several years after which they can be revived (Clark and Haskins, 2016). Despite these differences, one thing which all dormant spores (and more generally all dormant entities) have in common is that how long they can remain alive is limited. There is an interesting mirroring of the phenomenon of spore ageing and the kind of ageing that living entities undergo that the distinctions between *structura vivens*, living, and dead allow us to think about (see Figure 5).

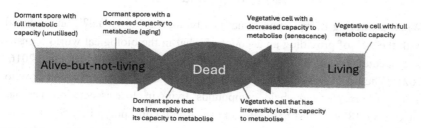

Figure 5 A mirroring of spore ageing and senescence in vegetative cells. The colour version of this figure is available at www.cambridge.org/Sims

---

[23] This assumes that the samples found were not contaminated.

A dormant spore's potential to metabolise changes over time and as such, spore ageing can be viewed as a decreasing capacity to metabolise. Spore death, on the other hand, is the complete loss of the capacity to metabolise. 'Senescence', ageing that is experienced exclusively by living entities, is characterised as the time-related loss of cellular growth, repair, and reproductive functions (Gilbert, 2000). Casting this loss of cellular function as a decreasing capacity to engage in metabolic exchange on the part of a living system, when living is conceptualised as a way of being alive, investigating spore ageing (and eventual spore death) may be a valuable proxy method for gaining insights into senescence. Setting aside the fact that different organisms have different senescence mechanisms (Bodnar, 2014), the question arises as to whether senescence may be underwritten by some of the same irreversible structural changes as spore ageing. For example, is cellular senescence accompanied by the same or similar kinds of protein structure modifying degradation that accompanies modification of protein structure in ageing spores? Another question is whether the same kinds of environmental factors that affect the progression of spore ageing might also affect the progression of senescence. In terms of practical implications, the possibility of using spore ageing in Physarum (or other spore bearing organisms) as an easy-to-study model system/phenomenon to investigate fundamental aspects of senescence in other taxa may very well be where the rubber meets the biological road. The DSVL taxonomy furnishes the conceptual distinctions to investigate this possibility.

Having made a case for how one particular stage of Physarum's complex life cycles (the spore) can be used as a starting point for thinking about the biotic status of spores more generally, let us now turn to another stage, the plasmodium, and a challenge that its fascinating behaviour poses for the notion of biological individuality.

4 Biological Individuals: A Puzzle Concerning Plasmodial Fragmenting and Fusing

When answering the question 'what is a biological individual?', one is faced with the task of providing an account of what in the biological world 'constitutes a countable, relatively well-delineated, and cohesive unit' (Pradeu, 2016: 762). Whether it was Charles Darwin's ([1839] 1967) concern about how to delineate barnacles and whale 'compounds' living in close association, Thomas Huxley's ([1859] 2008) befuddlement regarding coral polyp individuation, or Daniel Janzen's (1977) puzzlement over individuating clonally reproducing dandelions and aphids, it is clear that this question has perplexed biologists for (at least) nearly two centuries. Today, biological individuality continues to be a topic of joint interest to both biologists and philosophers of biology.

Various ways of addressing biological individuality have been developed in response to concerns, amongst other things, about how to distinguish specific cases of growth from reproduction and/or when a group of individuals no longer counts as a mere group but can be construed as an individual in its own right. Many times, such concerns have been motivated by puzzling cases from the biological world that challenge our folk intuitions about biological individuality. Are runner strawberry plants that are produced by and still connected to a main strawberry plant each individual's or are they distributed parts of the main plant? In addition to each member of a honeybee colony being an individual, is the colony itself an individual? In this tradition, here is a novel puzzle involving the behaviour of *P. polycephalum*.

A first observation: during Physarum's vegetative plasmodial stage (i.e., when they appear as a bright yellow mass of protoplasm), they have been observed to sometimes fragment into two separate, autonomous plasmodial cells. This happens, for example, when there are two spatially distanced food sources in a Petri dish and a single plasmodium fragments after reaching both (Nakagaki et al., 2000, 2001). A second observation: complete fusion of separate plasmodial cells has been observed to typically occur when plasmodia are closely related genetically, phenotypically identical (Clark and Haskins, 2012; Vogel and Dussutour, 2016), or, more generally, when they come from the same strain (Grey, 1945). Putting these two observations together, the possibility of an interesting conjunction of behavioural patterns arises.

Since both fragmentation and fusion are individually part of Physarum plasmodia's behavioural repertoire, there is little reason to think that fragmentation followed by fusion would not occur given the combination of experimental conditions that originally elicited fragmentation and fusion (e.g., a Petri dish of a certain size, the placement of food at different locations, and then wait for fusion to occur after food consumption). That said, the possibility of fragmentation followed by non-fusion cannot be completely ruled out either. Given that such a combined experiment, as far as I know, has yet to be performed, the possibility should be left open that fragmentation may be followed by non-fusion sometimes. Focusing on the plasmodial cell dyad – fragment pieces that we would expect to usually fuse but sometimes do not – a pressing question arises: is there any plausible reason to view the two spatially non-contiguous plasmodial cells as jointly constituting a biological individual in its own right?

The importance of various accounts and notions of biological individuality is heavily tied to different biological subdisciplines, their aims of inquiry, and respective methodological practices (Lidgard and Nyhart, 2017; Love and Brigandt, 2017). Different notions of individuality lead to different ways of counting the things that feature into the explanations of phenomena of interest. Addressing the question of whether the two plasmodial cells in the described combined experimental scenario jointly constitute a biological individual is grounded in myxomycete biology and may indeed be of value to this subdiscipline (or microbiology more generally). This value may lie in arriving at a more precise understanding of the kinds of behaviour that a single Physarum plasmodium is capable of in controlled laboratory settings. Admittedly, it is not telling of what a plasmodium does in its natural habitat. Another value may lie in something as fundamental as understanding when plasmodial fragmentation sometimes counts as reproduction and when it does not. Lastly, since the question is based upon an assumption about what would be likely to occur if two experiments were combined, it may prompt those interested biologists to investigate fragmentation and fusion patterns in the lab. This is a case in which the posing of a question about biological individuality may itself have some potential value to biology regardless of how it is answered.

In what follows, two different concepts of biological individual will be brought to bear on the question of whether the two plasmodial cell fragments in the described scenario jointly constitute a biological individual with the hope of gleaning some insight into plasmodial individuality. The respective concepts are those associated with what has been called *Darwinian individuals* and *metabolic individuals* (Godfrey-Smith, 2013a).[24] I will argue that the plasmodial dyad fails to qualify as a single Darwinian individual. On the other hand, taking fragmentation and fusion patterns into account may indeed warrant viewing the dyad as having *some degree* of metabolic individuality. This, however, requires expanding the 'orthodox' view of metabolic individuality in a way that does justice to the remarkable morphological and behavioural plasticity exhibited by a plasmodium.

This section will be organised as follows: firstly, I will describe the details of both Darwinian individuality and metabolic individuality. Using these notions of individuality, I will then evaluate the plasmodial dyad arriving at negative conclusion regarding its status as a Darwinian individuality. I shall then evaluate the dyad in terms of metabolic individuality, taking into account the larger behavioural context of fragmentation and fusion or non-fusion. After introducing a simple diagrammatic schema of plasmodial fragmentation-fusion and fragmentation-non-fusion patterns, I will argue that the possibility of the first of

---

[24] To be sure, Godfrey-Smith (2013a, 2013b) formulates an account of 'organisms' that is based upon the process of metabolism. To avoid any unnecessary confusion that might arise in adopting his specific use of the term, given how widely a more general notion of organism is used in this Element, in what follows I will continue to use 'metabolic individuals' to refer to Godfrey-Smith's 'organisms'.

these patterns happening at all requires rethinking the orthodox concept of metabolic individuality. Such a conceptual revision should reflect the fact that both fragmentation and fusion are metabolically beneficial behaviours. Given that fusion after fragmentation rules out reproduction by definition, the most parsimonious view is that there is one persisting, spatially oscillating metabolic individual across both fragmentation and fusion events. Lastly, I will articulate a counterfactual analysis of metabolic individuality specific to such cases of fragmentation and fusion in plasmodia or other organisms that possibly share this striking behavioural capacity.

4.1 Two Kinds of Biological Individual

In this section, I will review the notions of Darwinian individuality and metabolic individuality as developed and formulated by Godfrey-Smith (2009, 2013a).[25] I will focus upon these two specific types of biological individuals because they offer two very different individuality concepts that can be used to approach the puzzle of plasmodial fragmentation and fusion.[26]

4.1.1 Darwinian Individuals

Godfrey-Smith, in his seminal book *Darwinian Populations and Natural Selection* (2009) and in a series of papers published afterwards, develops one evolutionary notion of biological individuality that he calls 'Darwinian individuals'. According to Godfrey-Smith, Darwinian individuals are reproducing entities that are capable of forming parent–offspring lineages upon which natural selection can act. To unpack this notion, Godfrey-Smith uses a general definition of evolution by natural selection provided by Lewontin (1985). Accordingly, natural selection occurs whenever there is phenotypic *variation, heritability* of that variation from parent to offspring, and *differential reproductive success*. Thus, failing the capacity to reproduce and pass on variation means, an entity (or collective of entities) falls short of being a Darwinian individual in any sense.

Given the centrality of evolutionary theorising and evolutionary modelling in biology, the notion of Darwinian individuality is one that plays – at least implicitly – an important role therein (Clark, 2011; Lidgard and Nyhart, 2017). For example, being able to measure differential reproductive success and, hence, to predict how a phenotype might spread throughout a population requires being

---

[25] There have been numerous ways that the notion of biological individuality has been developed by both biologists and philosophers. For many such examples, see both (Clark, 2010) and (Lidgard and Nyhart, 2017).

[26] For a different analysis biological individuality that considers Physarum's ability to fuse after being split into different smaller individuals, see (Smith-Ferguson and Beekman, 2019).

able to count differences in the number of offspring produced by a parent/parents. Doing this presupposes an ability on the part of the counter to be able to distinguish both individuals that reproduce and offspring from parts of individuals that have resulted from mere growth (e.g., leaves of a plant) and groups of independently reproducing individuals (e.g., a school of fish or a field of dandelions). The notion of a Darwinian individual is meant to capture the appropriate countable *unit of reproduction* upon which evolution by natural selection acts. Darwinian individuals sometimes (but not always) map onto those individuals that are most easily discerned by us, those individuals – typically metazoans – that populate our folk biology (e.g., individual dogs, birds, humans, bees, etc.). That said, because there are many different kinds of reproducing, lineage forming entities, the notion of a Darwinian individual also applies to viruses, genes, chromosomes, and some collective entities (Godfrey-Smith, 2013a).

Recognising that modes of reproduction and reproducing units are both products of evolution and also how evolution occurs, Godfrey-Smith identifies three different types of reproducer. The first type, which he calls a 'scaffolded reproducer', is one that fails to have its own reproductive machinery and hence requires another system to reproduce itself. Viruses and genes are two examples. The second, a 'simple reproducer', is a Darwinian individual that can reproduce through its own resources and does not contain other reproducers like itself as component parts; that is, a simple reproducer does not contain other reproducers that are not themselves scaffolded reproducers. A paradigmatic example of a simple reproducer, he suggests, is a bacterium. A third type of reproducer is a 'collective reproducer'. Godfrey-Smith characterises such a reproducer as one that (non-exclusively) contains other reproducers of any of the three categories as constituent parts at lower levels of its organisational hierarchy.[27] We *Homo sapiens* and other multicellular organisms are collective reproducers since we are composed of reproducing bodily ('somatic') cells, but honeybee colonies are also collective reproducers to some degree (as will be soon explained).

Darwinian individuality has a gradient nature – an entity can be more or less of a Darwinian individual than another. A colony of honeybees qualifies as a Darwinian individual but less so than, say, a bird or a human. In the case of collective reproducers, Godfrey-Smith fleshes the graded nature of Darwinian individuality out in terms of the degree to which a collective's mode of reproduction exhibits three features: 'germlines', 'reproductive bottlenecks', and 'integration'. Whereas scoring high across all three features is characteristic of paradigmatic collectively reproducing Darwinian individuals, a low score

---

[27] Godfrey-Smith acknowledges the possibility of collective reproducers being made up of other collective reproducers, but rejects the idea that there can be collective reproducers 'all the way down' (2009: 88)

across all three features suggests the presence of a mere group. Darwinian individuals can fall anywhere in between these high or marginal scores. Let me briefly unpack each of these features in turn.

Germline refers to the presence of *a division of reproductive labour* amongst the different entities in a collective. Germ cells in mammals, for example, are the only cells from which the same kind of organism can be reproductively derived. Mammalian somatic cells, on the other hand, can reproductively give rise to only differentiated cells like themselves and not an entire organism. A colony of honey bees also has a certain degree of reproductive specialisation, their different castes functioning analogously to germ and soma cells in mammals in important ways. Reproduction of the colony is limited to queens and male drones, whereas female workers are functionally sterile. A division of reproductive labour is a mechanism that ensures that selection occurs at the level of the collective individual (e.g., the individual human or honeybee colony) as opposed to independent selection occurring also at the level of its nested parts (e.g., somatic cells or the individual honeybee); it de-Darwinises lower-level units (Godfrey-Smith, 2009).

Godfrey-Smith characterises a reproductive bottleneck as a narrowing that marks the start of a new generation in a life cycle, something that often takes the form of a single cell. Bottlenecks serve as a mechanism to introduce variation into the next generation given that small genetic changes in a single cell can result in significant downstream effects over the course of development. Like germ-lines, bottlenecks are a matter of degree. Lastly, integration refers to a more general kind of division of labour that is characteristically exhibited to greater or lesser degrees by collective reproducers. It is a division of labour other than that of a reproductive division of labour. For instance, integration may take the form of 'the mutual dependence of parts, and the maintenance of a boundary between a collective and what is outside it' (Godfrey-Smith, 2013a: 21). Interestingly, Godfrey-Smith (2013a) sees behaviour-coordinating chemical communication and waggle dances that occur between honeybees as counting towards the colony having some degree of integration, suggesting that spatial contiguity is only one manner of being integrated (also see Herron, 2017).

Germlines, bottlenecks, and integration are features of one kind of Darwinian individual – a collective reproducer. Both simple and scaffolded reproducers represent other kinds of Darwinian individuals that, like collective reproducers, speak of degrees of Darwinian individuality.

4.1.2 Metabolic Individuals

Another way that biological individuals have been conceptualised is not tethered to evolutionary theory or reproduction; rather, it is physiology (i.e., the study of the various mechanisms that allow biological systems to maintain themselves despite fluctuation in environmental conditions) that biological individuality is tied to. Metabolic integration is one way that physiological individuality has been fleshed out historically (J. Huxley, [1912] 2022) and continues to be a central concept for approaching difficult questions regarding biological individuality.[28] One such question is concerned with 'mutualist symbiotic associations' – an association of two or more heterospecific organisms that each benefit from their reciprocal interactions. For example, *Vibrio fischeri* bacteria colonise the internal cavity of the Bobtail squid (*Euprymna scolopes*), feeding upon mucus produced by the squid. In turn, as the density of the bacterial colony grows, *V. fischeri* begin to luminesce as a result of quorum sensing, allowing the glowing and shadowless squid to hunt undetected by predators or prey. At dawn, the squid expels most bacteria. As it rests over the day, the remaining colony repopulate its cavity, and the cycle begins anew.[29] Does such a squid–bacterial association count as a metabolic individual – if only a temporary one – in its own right? Answering such a question seems important if not for the fact that symbiotic associations are ubiquitous in nature – one of which includes us and our various gut bacteria (Dupre and O'Malley, 2009; Gilbert et al., 2018), but also because symbiosis is thought to have played a central role in the evolutionary transition from prokaryotes to eukaryotes (Maynard-Smith and Szathmary, 1995).

It is now generally acknowledged that the prokaryote–eukaryote transition resulted from a prokaryote cell (an archaeon) engulfing another (a bacterium) and, rather than consuming it, the host cell benefited from the engulfed cell's metabolic by-products and simultaneously provided a stable environment for the engulfed cell to maintain itself over time.[30] The mutual metabolic integration of both the engulfed cell and the host cell provides a plausible explanation as to how the tight interaction between two (Darwinian) individuals may have resulted in the evolution of a new kind of (Darwinian) individual – a new unit of selection. Thus, the formation of a metabolic individual (e.g., an endosymbiont bacterium and its host archaeon) was a precursory stage on the way to a new unit of reproduction (i.e., a eukaryote). Although metabolic individuality is not

---

[28] See (Pradeu, 2016) for another manner of fleshing out physiology-based biological individuality in terms of immune tolerance.

[29] For a comprehensive overview of Bobtail squid and *V. fischeri* symbiosis, see (McFall-Ngai, 2014).

[30] This is a general description of endosymbiotic theory, the renewed interest of which in evolutionary biology can be accredited to Lynn Sagan (1967) – thereafter known as Lynn Margulis. Today, it is accepted by most biologists that cellular mitochondria (the 'metabolic powerhouses' found within all eukaryotic cells) are derived from an ancient endosymbiotic event in which a bacterium was engulfed by archaeon cell giving rise to an ancestral eukaryote. See Martin et al. (2015) for further details about the endosymbiotic origins of eukaryotes.

tethered to evolutionary theory, it provides one valuable way of thinking about how certain new types of Darwinian individuals came (and perhaps continue to come) into being. So, what is a metabolic individual?

Let us begin by focusing on what they are not. Metabolic individuals needn't (but can) be the kinds of things that reproduce; in contrast to Darwinian individuals, reproduction is only a contingent feature (Godfrey-Smith, 2009). One result of this is that metabolic individuals can have any evolutionary history, something that opens up a theoretical space to consider how metabolically integrated entities that cannot form parent–offspring lineages together can nevertheless qualify as more than a mere collection of independent entities. This is one reason why metabolic individuals can potentially play a role in understanding how some new Darwinian individuals could have emerged in the first place (e.g., unicellular eukaryotes with their endosymbiont mitochondria).

Now, to positive characterisation: according to Godfrey-Smith, metabolic individuals are

> systems comprised of diverse parts which work together to maintain the system's structure, despite turnover of material, by making use of sources of energy and other resources from their environment. (2013a: 25)

According to this view – what I shall continue to refer to as the 'orthodox view' – metabolic individuals are systems made up of heterogeneous parts, the nature of which allows for some kind of functional (metabolic) integration to arise between them. Having diverse parts amounts to systems possessing *different features and capacities* (e.g., morphology, biochemical responses, behaviours, etc.) that constrain mutually supportive metabolic interaction. Thus, we can think of the parts of a metabolic individual as exhibiting a *division of metabolic labour* (e.g., the *V. fischeri* luminesce and contribute to the bobtailed squid's bioluminescent camouflage, whilst the squid provides mucus food and a reproduction conducive environment for the bacteria).

Importantly, the orthodox view emphasises that the diverse parts of a metabolic individual must function together in the service of *maintaining the individual*. That is, such individuals 'are essentially persisters, systems that use energy to resist the forces of decay, and only contingently things that reproduce' (Godfrey-Smith, 2013a: 25). One way that a metabolic individual is maintained, according to Godfrey-Smith, is in virtue of *cooperation* between its parts (see also Queller and Strassman, 2009). I think it is fair to interpret Godfrey-Smith as viewing cooperation as a specification of the type of metabolism-relevant integration that occurs between the parts of a metabolic individual that contribute to its persistence. Since such cooperation is a matter of degree, metabolic individuality is itself a gradient notion (Godfrey-Smith, 2009). Without more than a marginal degree of metabolism-relevant integration, a collection of entities is no more than a group of spatially localised members. Such integration is illustrated in the case of the bobtail-*V. fischeri*- mutualistic symbiosis, where the squid–bacteria association is maintained nightly as a camouflaged, hunting unit in virtue of the activities of both symbionts.

Cooperation via metabolic division of labour places no demand on metabolic individuality with respect to spatial contiguity. As long as the parts of a collection are interactively organised so as to allow for effective metabolic cooperation, two or more spatially non-contiguous entities may nonetheless qualify as a joint individual that is maintained over time. That said, however, the further apart the constituent parts are in space, the weaker their cooperative interactions are and as a result, the more marginal the metabolic individuality of the joint system is (Godfrey-Smith, 2013b).

Crucially, in order for highly cooperating parts that are also metabolic individuals themselves to become a joint metabolic individual, some degree of their metabolic independence must be partially or temporarily 'surrendered' for that of the higher-level metabolic individual or as Godfrey-Smith writes:

> If a whole system has a highly organismal form of integration, if it is a whole with respect to its metabolic activity, then its parts must, necessarily, be less organismal [less of a metabolic individual]. Those parts must be highly interdependent, less able to function as metabolic whole themselves. (2013a: 26; my insertion)

And conversely, if the parts of a system exhibit a high degree of independence with respect to maintaining themselves metabolically, this reduces the degree to which the joint system they comprise qualifies as a metabolic individual. Whilst inside the squid, *V. fischeri* are highly dependent on the squid for food; the nocturnal hunting success of the bobtail on the other hand is dependent on the bacteria, during the period of the diel cycle in which the bacteria populate the squid's cavity. When the squid expels most of the bacteria in the morning, it and any given expelled bacterium (or bacteria) are metabolically independent again and thus no longer jointly qualify as a metabolic individual.

There is one last important aspect of Godfrey-Smith's analysis of biological individuals that is worth mentioning: although there are cases in which biological individuals are either a metabolic individual *or* a Darwinian individual, there can be biological individuals that are both (see also Ereshefsky and Pedroso, 2015). For example, whereas a gene is a Darwinian individual but not a metabolic individual, a bobtail squid–*V. fischeri* symbiotic association is a metabolic individual but not a Darwinian individual (i.e., there is no parent–offspring lineage common to both symbionts because they reproduce independently). On the other hand, a honeybee colony may not only qualify as a Darwinian individual to some degree but, given that the colony is a metabolically integrated system with a division of metabolic labour among its interacting bee parts, it may also be viewed as exhibiting a non-zero degree of metabolic individuality (cf. Seeley, 1989).

Having reviewed Darwinian and Metabolic individuals, let us now turn to the task of evaluating whether the plasmodial dyad in the cases of fragmenting and fusion (or non-fusion) qualifies as either a Darwinian individual and/or a metabolic individual.

4.2 Evaluating the Plasmodial Dyad

Recall the possible behavioural patterns described earlier: a single plasmodium fragments into two separate cells after reaching two spatially separate food sources. Subsequent to consuming the food sources, these cells are likely to fuse, forming one larger plasmodial cell. The puzzle to be addressed is whether the plasmodial dyad is a biological individual above and beyond the two plasmodial cells which the dyad consists of.

Let us start with considering whether the dyad counts as a Darwinian individual (or has some degree of Darwinian individuality). A plasmodium is a unicellular multinucleate organism. During cell growth, its nuclei continuously reproduce via mitosis without cell division. However, unlike bodily cell division, which can occur independently of the particular extracellular milieu (e.g., in a Petri dish), nuclear division cannot occur outside of the cell environment. This suggests that Physarum nuclei are scaffolded reproducers according to Godfrey-Smith's framework. Since it only contains scaffolded reproducers, a single plasmodial cell qualifies as a simple reproducer. Given that only collective reproducers can themselves be made up of other entities that can make more of themselves by way of their own reproductive 'machinery' (i.e., collective, and/or simple reproducers), a collective reproducer is the most reasonable option of the three reproducer categories to base an evaluation of the plasmodial dyad upon. Rephrasing the question above more precisely in terms of Darwinian individuals: is the plasmodial dyad a collective reproducer (at least to some degree) that is composed of simple reproducers?

One reason to answer this question negatively is that the two plasmodial cells, despite being genetic clones, are independent lineage formers. Thus, there is no feature that unites them as a collective reproducer. To see this, consider the features that Godfrey-Smith introduces to adjudicate collectively reproducing

Darwinian individuals. The two plasmodial cells score null for germ line; there is no division of reproductive labour that the two spatially separate cells exhibit; each cell is able to reproduce and do so independently of the other. The dyad has a similar score for both reproductive bottleneck (a narrowing that marks the beginning of a new generation) and integration (i.e., spatial boundedness).[31] These scores across all three features suggest that the dyad is not itself a collective lineage-forming system. In other words, the dyad is a mere group and not the kind of thing that reproduces as a unit and/or takes part in the process of evolution by natural selection. Does the plasmodial dyad stand a better chance of exhibiting some degree of metabolic individuality?

This question boils down to one of whether or not the two plasmodial cells engage in some degree of metabolic cooperation. At first blush, it seems that neither member of the plasmodial dyad reciprocally interacts with the other, metabolically integrating in the service of the dyad's continued existence. One might expect this to be the case since the two plasmodia making up the dyad, unlike, say, symbiotic associations or different honeybee castes, are homogeneous members that share the same features (i.e., clones). Accordingly, it might be thought that neither plasmodial fragment cell can provide the other with something that it cannot already provide itself and thus interaction between homogeneous parts does not lend itself to a cooperative metabolic division of labour (cf. Godfrey-Smith, 2013a). This, however, I would like to argue is too fast. In the next section, I will show that limiting the evaluation to the features of the dyad in isolation from what occurs prior (fragmentation) and subsequent to it (fusion or non-fusion) obscures the big picture – a picture which is necessary for recognising potential instances of at least one unusual form of metabolic individuality. Seeing the big picture means recognising patterns of plasmodial behaviour as they occur over time, taking more generally what has become known as a processual view of biological individuality (see Meincke and Dupré, 2020).

4.2.1 Fragmentation, Fusion, and Non-fusion Patterns

The two different plasmodial behavioural patterns that will be used in what follows to evaluate metabolic individuality in plasmodia I will call *fragmentation-fusion* (FF) and *fragmentation-non-fusion* (FN) patterns. I have included simplified diagrammatic schemas of FF and FN in Figure 6. The first pattern, FF, represents one initial plasmodial cell at t^1 that spreads out and covers two spatially distant food sources at t^2. After a period of consuming food, the t^2 cell fragments into two

---

[31] The dyad is not a bottleneck since it is a doubling in cell number relative to the fragmenting plasmodium.

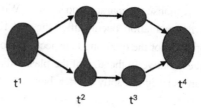

Figure 6 Plasmodial fragmentation-fusion (FF) schema: arrows represent different events. The first set of arrows represent a spreading event that results in a one distributed plasmodial cell that covers both food sources at t^2. The second set of arrows represents fragmentation event that results in two spatially separate plasmodial cells at each food source location at t^3. The third set of arrows represents a fusion event in which the dyad at t^3 merge to form a single plasmodial cell at t^4. The colour version of this figure is available at www.cambridge.org/Sims

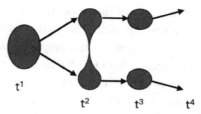

Figure 7 Plasmodial fragmentation-non-fusion (FN) Schema: all events up to t^3 are identical to FF. The third set of arrows represents non-fusion event. The colour version of this figure is available at www.cambridge.org/Sims

fully separate cells at t^3 that continue to consume the two food sources independently. After the food has been consumed, the t^3 cells fuse at t^4 (see Figure 6).

The second pattern, FN, is identical to FF except that the two plasmodia, after consuming the separate food sources at t^3, do not fuse at t^4 but continue to live as independent cells (see Figure 7). One result of what I am calling non-fusion is that the two cells become resource competitors. This can even potentially lead to one of the two cells consuming the other (see Clark and Haskins, 2012).

I will now show how evaluating the metabolic individuality of plasmodial dyad in the larger contexts of FF and FN reveals an interesting possibility that is consistent with viewing the dyad at t^3 as a spatially non-contiguous metabolic individual. Let's put some flesh on the bones of this way of looking at FF and FN.

4.2.2 Evaluation of the Dyad in the Context of FF and FN Patterns

Recall that fragmentation between t^2 and t^3 occurs after a plasmodial cell has reached and partially consumed, spatially separated food sources. Thus, fragmentation is a behaviour that occurs in response to separate food sources. What kinds of conditions would affect whether fragmentation occurs after the cell reaches the two food sources? One condition, but not the only one I suspect, has to do with the distance between the food sources relative to the size of the plasmodial cell. If the distance separating the food sources is significantly shorter than the size of the cell, then the cell could cover both sources without needing to extend itself in any manner. On the other hand, if the distance between the food sources is significantly greater than the overall size of the cell, then to cover and consume both sources simultaneously, the cell must plastically modify its shape to reach both sources. It is only in this latter 'stretched out' case that fragmentation would seem to benefit the cell in exploiting both resources. In other words, 'network shape is the solution to the organism's survival problems' (Nakagaki et al., 2004: 2305).

If the cell at t^1 can reach both food sources by altering its morphology and connecting the two sources, what is the benefit of fragmenting? One possible answer, and not the only one, is that the shuttling of protoplasm between the spatially distributed regions of the plasmodial cell when it has covered both food sources is metabolically expensive and may slow down the process of consuming each of the sources of food (cf. Nakagaki et al., 2004); that is, in certain foraging landscapes two smaller cells may be more efficient at consuming each food source simultaneously than a larger stretched-out cell is. Therefore, if fragmentation offers a benefit that is contingent upon both the size of the cell and the length of the distance between the food sources, then fragmentation in response to food may be viewed as a behavioural strategy for efficient food consumption.

Fragmentation in plasmodia, when extending across two distant food sources, is driven by changes in internal protoplasmic shuttling (Section 2) that reallocate cytoplasm, nutrients, and other cellular components towards separate growth regions (Nakagaki et al., 2001). With reduced protoplasmic flow between the two regions that are in contact with the food, the vein-like tubule that connects them decays, resulting in the fragmenting of the cell. Does this mean that fragmentation is something that happens to the cell, rather than something that the cell actively does? There is a compelling reason to think that fragmentation is, in fact, under the cell's behavioural control. Protoplasmic shutting is how a plasmodium normally locomotes, in addition to how it forages and explores its environment. It is an underlying behavioural mechanism. As such, the fact that changes in protoplasmic shuttling underwrite fragmentation fails to be a reason to view fragmenting as something other than controlled behaviour – any more than it is a reason to deny that locomotion, foraging, or exploring are controlled behaviours. Fragmenting in this case is something that a plasmodial cell does and not something that merely happens to it.

Thus far, the description of the behavioural pattern, from t^1 to t^3, is common to both FF and FN. The difference between the two patterns is paramount to evaluating plasmodial metabolic individuality. In the case of FF, the two cells of the dyad fuse at t^4. This is something that would be expected to occur given that the cells originated from the same larger cell (i.e., they are genetic clones) and that no mutations accumulated in the short period of time since fragmentation, rendering them too genetically different to fuse (cf. Clark and Haskins, 2012). What is relevant here is that fusion can occur at t^4 because the cells of the dyad are clones (closely genetically related if not identical). When the two cells fuse, something interesting happens. The cell boundary separating the two adjacent cells begins to degrade and the protoplasm shuttling tubules from each cell begins to connect with the other cell's tubules. As this occurs, the 'fruit' of each cell's metabolic labour is reciprocally shared as protoplasm flows through the connecting tubules. During the final step of complete fusion, the two cells can no longer be distinguished from the larger plasmodial cell that they become; the cells lose their metabolic (and Darwinian) individuality for that of the larger plasmodial cell they become at t^4.

Recall that metabolic individuals persist over time despite turnover of materials and, more generally, change. Varying degrees of metabolic integration of interacting parts (i.e., cooperation) is the functional 'glue' of the persisting individual. The plasmodial cell at t^1 and at t^2, respectively, have high degrees of metabolic cooperation amongst their intracellular parts. Similarly, the fused plasmodial cell at t^4 is also a highly metabolically integrated unit. It is not immediately obvious, on the other hand, how each cell of the dyad at t^3 may metabolically cooperate with the other given the fact that each cell's metabolic machinery is highly autonomous. On closer inspection and when placed in the context of FF, however, there is a precursory process which enables subsequent metabolic integration and is mediated by the shared environmental substrate that the two cells occupy. Although this precursory process is not itself *direct* metabolic integration (it does not affect either cells' metabolic activity), it counts as a form of *indirect metabolic integration* when placed in the context of FF. How might this be the case?

Plasmodia exude various biochemicals such as calcium into the substrate upon which they locomote and rest (Vogel et al., 2015; Briard et al., 2020). In a lab setting, this substrate is typically 'agar' (i.e., a non-living gelatinous substance that is derived from seaweed) that covers the bottom of a Petri dish. It has been shown that biochemicals that diffuse into a substrate can be used as cues by those plasmodia which detect them to guide their navigational behaviour. More precisely, if the plasmodium which leaves the biochemical cue is stressed (e.g., starved), then the cue will elicit an aversion response on the part of the plasmodium that detects it. On the other hand, if the plasmodium that exudes the biochemical is well-nourished, then the cue acts as an attractant. Being an attractant means that a plasmodium that detects it will be likely to approach the source of the diffusing biochemical gradient (Vogel et al., 2015; Briard et al., 2020). Sometimes this source will be the plasmodium that left the cue.

With this in mind, and returning to FF, if each separate plasmodial cell that consumes the spatially separate food sources exudes a cue that acts as an attractant (or a repellent) for the other, relaying the condition of the plasmodium that left the cue, then it seems that in addition to genetic similarity, the physiological condition of the two plasmodia can affect whether or not they fuse. Given the use of *environment-mediated* chemical cues that lead to fusion of the two cells in FF, I would like to suggest that there is a sense in which the two separate cells have a degree of indirect metabolic integration.[32] Importantly, such indirect integration occurs only when both plasmodial cells leave and use cues that are attractive and, as a result, pave the way for subsequent fusion to occur.[33] In this sense, calcium may play a similar role in indirectly integrating spatially separate plasmodia as autoinducers produced by *V. fischeri* during quorum-sensing play in indirectly integrating bacteria and bobtail squid prior to bioluminescence of the squid–*Vibrio* individual.

Putting all of the pieces together: the occurrence of fragmentation followed by fusion, FF, I would like to argue, licenses viewing fusion as the reforming of the plasmodial cell that fragmented. The plasmodial dyad, if this is correct, despite being homogeneous parts, represent a *spatial* division of metabolic labour on the part of the fragmenting plasmodium. When the plasmodium at t^2 fragments, it persists as a higher-level metabolic individual comprised of the two cells (lower-level metabolic individuals), metabolically benefiting as a unit from the behaviour of each of its non-contiguous parts only *after fusion*. There is a degree of indirect metabolic integration between the two separate plasmodial cells at t^3. However, and in contrast to the orthodox view of metabolic individuality, what matters most in the case of FF is that the fruit of each cell's metabolic labour is shared during subsequent fusion. If this is correct, then FF represents an interesting case in which an initially high degree of direct metabolic integration of the plasmodial cell at t^1 and t^2 is *temporarily interrupted* at t^3 and then subsequently *re-established* at t^4. This temporary interruption also means a substantial temporary decrease in the degree of metabolic independence (and hence metabolic individuality) of the persisting higher-level dyadic

---

[32] See Seeley (1989) on honeybee colony integration via cues and shared environment.

[33] It follows that such indirect metabolic integration would not occur if the two cells were separated by a large distance or if they were unable to detect and respond to each other's cues.

individual during the period in which it is only indirectly integrated. In contrast, each cell of the dyad that is produced as a result of fragmentation has a high degree of metabolic independence (and metabolic individuality) until they fuse.

This temporary interruption of the initially high degree of direct metabolic integration and its re-establishment can be viewed as an exhibition of plastic, metabolism-driven behaviour on the part of the fragmenting individual – a metabolic individual that is maintained over FF despite being spatially non-contiguous. The phenotypic plasticity exhibited by Physarum at the various stages across its life cycle, as we saw in Section 2, and the highly plastic behaviour of plasmodia in particular (as documented by Nakagaki et al., 2001; Dussutour et al., 2010; Latty and Beekman, 2011; Vogel and Dussutour, 2016), provide some additional support for this interpretation, at least in theory.

Lastly, what about FN – something that cannot be ruled out from occurring a priori? When fusion fails to occur after the cells of the dyad have consumed the separate food sources, we may infer that a full loss of indirect metabolic integration has occurred during t^3. In failing to fuse, the fruit of each of the cell's metabolic labour cannot be shared but is instead used by each cell independently as it becomes a resource competitor with the other. Thus, whether the dyad qualifies as a metabolic individual is contingent upon the occurrence of FF, something which is underwritten by environment-mediated indirect metabolic integration.

This kind evaluation may not sit right with some. One might argue that in the case of FF it is more intuitive to view the fragmenting individual as ceasing to exist after fragmentation, with a *new* metabolic individual being created when and only when the two resulting cells fuse at a later time. While this alternative evaluation may seem intuitive, its being so is less indicative of its correctness and more indicative of the fact that the forms which metabolic individuals take can often strain our intuitions. The ease with which our intuitions can change and pull in opposite directions under slightly different conditions illustrate that they are not a reliable metric for determining all cases of biological individuality. For example, our intuitive sense of whether the same pre-fragmentation individual persists during the separation and after fusion may depend on the duration of separation. If FF occurs over hours, it might intuitively seem that the fragmenting individual does not persist. However, if FF would occur over a period of seconds, we might intuit the opposite. This inconsistency raises the questions: how long must the two cells be apart before the pre-fragmenting and post-fusion plasmodia are considered distinct individuals? How quickly must they fuse to qualify as a single continuous individual? The lack of clear, non-arbitrary answers suggests that intuition alone is not a reliable guide when it comes to such a case of metabolic individuality (or biological individuality more generally). Although the evaluation that I have proposed may be less intuitive than the alternative, this by itself is no reason to prefer the latter.[34]

One might still object that, regardless of differences in intuitions, this evaluation unnecessarily multiplies metabolic individuals in a way that the simpler alternative does not, thus dulling Occam's razor. The proposed evaluation posits three coexisting metabolic individuals after fragmentation (the two separate cells of the dyad and the joint individual that they constitute), whereas the alternative posits only two (each cell of the dyad). Although simplicity is generally viewed as a value in scientific explanation and evaluation, it does not necessarily mean that simpler evaluations (or explanations) are always preferable. In the context of biological individuality, the notion of simplicity must be approached with caution. Take for example the symbiotic association between the bobtail squid and *V. fischeri*: if one considers this – as many philosophers of biology do – a transient metabolic individual, one implicitly acknowledges a nested individual, the existence of which is above and beyond that of the squid and its numerous bacterial symbionts. All such analyses of symbiotic associations, however, are rendered dead in the water if simpler evaluations are viewed as inherently superior. Moreover, the very question of whether a symbiotic association is a metabolic individual (or a Darwinian individual) turns out to be ill-posed under the assumption the simpler evaluations trump all others. Given that we continue to pose interesting questions about metabolic individuality regarding systems like symbiotic associations – questions that play a role in legitimate scientific theorising – I do not see why the plausibility of the proposed evaluation should be dismissed because it is less simple than the alternative.[35]

4.3 Moving Beyond the Orthodoxy

Taking the proposed evaluation onboard requires expanding the orthodox view of metabolic individuals and rethinking how metabolic independence (autonomy) is exhibited at different adjacent levels of a biological hierarchy. In the orthodox account of metabolic individuality that I have described, it is par for the course to evaluate whether some group of metabolic individuals is a higher-level, collective metabolic individual by taking into account the metabolic

---

[34] Perhaps the idea that a metabolic individual is spatially non-contiguous is one source of discomfort with the proposed solution. It should be remembered, however, that this idea is not by any means a unique feature of the particular solution that I have argued for; it is generally acknowledged that metabolic individuals can be spatially non-contiguous. Ant colonies are one such example that will be explored in Section 5.

[35] Many thanks to an anonymous reviewer for encouraging me to discuss this alternative way of evaluating FF.

integration of its constituent parts. What is not taken into account, however, is whether the constituent parts have a *shared beginning* and whether or not it is typical for those parts to have a *shared end*. More precisely, the evaluation of metabolic individuality that is typical of the orthodox view does not take into account whether the entities being evaluated are the products of fragmentation and whether those entities are likely to fuse together subsequent to exercising their independent metabolic machinery.

Perhaps one reason for this is that the problem cases for metabolic individuality (or more generally for physiological individuality) that philosophers and biologists have tended to focus on evaluating have often taken the form of symbiotic associations of various calibres. Symbionts, being heterospecific, are not themselves the products of fragmentation events of a monospecific organism. Another reason may be as simple as rarity of occurrence. Although asexual reproduction via fragmentation is common in a number of taxa ranging from some plants, animals, and fungi, what is much less common is the combination of organism-initiated fragmentation and subsequent fusion of those fragments.[36] In the case of FN, absence of fusion suggests that FN events end up being an instance of asexual reproduction. When the combination of fragmenting and subsequent fusion occurs, fragmentation may be seen as a form of plastic, metabolism-driven behaviour. Physarum plasmodia (and myxomycetes more generally) may be unique in exhibiting both fragmentation and fusion. Assuming that the FF pattern would occur given that fragmentation and fusion occur separately, the orthodox notion of metabolic individual may be stretched to its limit in this particular case.

4.4 A Counterfactual Metabolic Analysis

If I am correct, contextualising the dyad suggests that metabolic integration can sometimes take a different form from that which is often the focus of the orthodox view of metabolic individuality; it can be indirect. Evaluating this different form of integration is ultimately tied up with knowing *what happens next* in the sequence of events, knowing whether or not fusion occurs after fragmentation. In this sense, whether FF or FN occurs determines whether the plasmodial dyad is or is not a joint metabolic individual. Although metabolic integration between the cells is indirect during the period in which they are separate, what matters in this case is that their independent metabolic activities contribute to the larger biological individual that they jointly maintain.

---

[36] Sponges can fuse sometimes when conditions are suitable after fragmentation due to damage. However, since it is damage that causes fragmentation rather than something that the sponge itself does in response to separate food sources, such a pattern differs significantly from FF.

It is only after the two cells have fused – if they do – that we can look back at their behaviour as representing a division of metabolic labour that the higher-level individual comprised of the two cells benefits from as a unit. Thus, whether or not the dyad is a metabolic individual is contingent upon what would occur after fragmentation. I would like to suggest that when adjudicating the metabolic individuality of the dyad at t^3 without knowing what happens next, the best we can settle for is a counterfactual analysis. This may take something like the following form:

> **Counterfactual analysis of metabolic individuality**: if fusion of two plasmodial cells originating from the same fragmenting plasmodium would occur sometime after food resource exploitation, then the two plasmodial cells qualify as a single metabolic individual.

Importantly, that fusion is not guaranteed to occur subsequent to fragmentation (although it is likely) calls important attention to the idea that evaluation of metabolic individuality must sometimes occur on a *case-by-case basis*. While the best method that we may be able to deploy when considering the metabolic individuality of any fragmented plasmodium cell prior to its fusing (or not fusing) is a counterfactual analysis, the actual evaluation of metabolic individuality must be made a posteriori and does not generalise to all cases. Thus, the puzzle of plasmodial fragmentation and fusion has a backwards-facing solution.

Turning to the next and final section of this Element, we shall look at another fascinating instance of highly plastic plasmodial behaviour – one that has gained the interest of biologists, philosophers, and cognitive scientists: the use of extracellular slime trails for navigating complex environments.

5 Externalised Spatial Memory?

Over the last two decades, Physarum has become a model system for investigating the possibility of various cognitive capacities in non-neuronal organisms (Dussutour, 2021; Reid, 2023). One motivation for carrying out such studies is made explicit in the increasingly popular research programme of 'basal cognition' (Lyon et al., 2021). The idea behind basal cognition is to investigate potential exercises of capacities such as learning, memory, anticipation, and decision making in non-neuronal organisms with the aim of identifying shared mechanisms that underwrite both complex cognitive capacities found in animals and those simpler capacities found in non-neuronal organisms.[37] For

---

[37] In what follows, I will assume the following working definition of cognition: 'Cognition comprises the sensory and other information-processing mechanisms an organism has for becoming familiar with, valuing, and interacting productively with features of its environment [exploring, exploiting, evading] in order to meet existential needs, the most basic of which are

example, it is posited that some mechanisms underwriting neuronal information processing may be highly evolutionarily conserved, dating back to similar mechanisms in early free-living cells (Levin, 2019). Moreover, there is the live possibility that functionally similar cognitive capacities that are exhibited in a wide range of organisms could be the result of convergent evolution (Dussutour, 2021). Thus, one way of approaching the study of cognition and cognition-like capacities (but by no means the only way) is to examine instances in which simple organisms like Physarum flexibly and adaptively direct their behaviour in response to sensed changes in environmental conditions.

Numerous studies looking in particular at the behaviour of Physarum plasmodia have shown that they exhibit various capacities to process information that have been hitherto only observed in animals. Despite lacking either a nervous system and/or a fixed shape, individual plasmodial cells have been observed to find the shortest path between food sources in different legs of a maze (Nakagaki et al., 2000), to become habituated to aversive stimuli (a simple form of learning) (Dussutour, 2021), to make complex foraging decisions (Latty and Beekman, 2011), and to engage in a form of anticipatory behaviour (Saigusa et al., 2008). These results suggest that a plasmodium does not mechanically and invariably respond to its environment by way of stimulus-response pathways; rather, it evaluates multiple environmental conditions that it encounters and uses those evaluations to flexibly guide its behaviour in ways that are consistent with its continued viability.

One capacity that has garnered the attention of both biologists and philosophers, something that was briefly mentioned in Section 2, is Physarum's ability to use its secreted extracellular slime to direct its navigation in a way that allows it to avoid revisiting previously foraged areas (Reid et al., 2012). Some researchers have proposed that extracellular slime functions as an externalised spatial memory for plasmodia when navigating through complex environments (Reid et al., 2012; Smith-Ferguson et al., 2017; Sims and Kiverstein, 2022). This interpretation challenges the conventional view of memory in cognitive science and psychology as being an *internally* stored structure (e.g., an 'engram', trace, etc.) – a structure traditionally associated in neuronal organisms with strengthened synaptic connections and, more recently (and more contentiously), associated with macromolecules such as non-coding RNA in both neuronal and non-neuronal organisms (see Gershman, 2023). Setting this internalist assumption aside, in this section, I would like to focus upon two primary questions about the relationship between memory, cognition,

---

survival/persistence, growth/ thriving, and reproduction' (Lyon et al., 2021: 4). Awareness, on this characterisation, is not a requirement of cognition.

and learning raised by the cognitive interpretation of Physarum's interaction with its extracellular slime. More precisely, such an interpretation prompts us to consider what makes memory a part of a cognitive process (i.e., subject to cognitive explanation), and whether memory always results from some form of learning. Using Reid et al.'s experiment as a jumping off point, it is my aim in this section to show how addressing each of these questions can be informative about addressing the other.

This section will be organised as follows: firstly, I will describe the details of Reid et al.'s (2012) experiment. Then I will consider the two primary questions regarding memory's relation to learning and cognition that Physarum's interaction with its extracellular slime brings to the fore. After suggesting one way of differentiating memory that is subject to cognitive explanation from that which is not using degrees of metabolic individuality (Section 4), four different categories of biological memory will be articulated and used to construct a fourfold memory analysis. Lastly, this analysis will be used to situate Reid et al.'s experimental results.

5.1 Reid et al.'s 2012 Physarum Experiment

A notable characteristic of plasmodia is their tendency to leave behind a visible residue of extracellular slime as it moves through its environment. Taking this into account, Reid et al. posed the question of whether a Physarum plasmodium, upon encountering extracellular slime, employs it as a guide to steer away from previously explored areas that may have been depleted of nutrients. To investigate this question, these researchers conducted experiments under two different conditions to assess how the use of extracellular slime influenced the speed of a plasmodium in successfully reaching a food source (glucose). In the first condition (referred to as the 'blank' condition), they lined the Petri dish with untreated agar, placing a drop of glucose solution (the 'goal') on top. As it defused within the agar, this glucose created an attraction gradient that the plasmodium could follow to navigate to the food source. A U-shaped acetate trap was then positioned on the agar's surface between the food source and the starting point of the plasmodium. Since plasmodia do not move as efficiently over dry surfaces, this dry acetate trap acted as an obstacle to reaching the glucose source. In the second condition (referred to as the 'coated' condition), the set-up was the same except that the agar was coated with a layer of extracellular slime. In both conditions, Reid et al. measured the time it took for Physarum to successfully reach the goal.

The researchers hypothesised that if extracellular slime was indeed used by Physarum to avoid revisiting previously explored areas, then the time taken to reach the food source would be significantly longer in the coated condition compared to the blank condition. This is because the slime-treated agar would obscure the plasmodium's own extracellular slime tracks. Remarkably, Reid et al. discovered that the average time that a plasmodium spent migrating across areas of agar it had previously explored was nearly ten times longer in the coated condition than in the blank condition. According to Reid et al., these findings 'offer a unique demonstration of a spatial memory system in a non-neuronal organism, supporting the theory that an externalised spatial memory may be the functional precursor to the internal memory of higher organisms' (2012: 1). Is extracellular slime really memory, and if so, is it the kind of memory that is significant to the study of cognition?

Here is one working definition of biological memory offered by biologists Frantisek Baluška and Michael Levin:

> Memory is defined as experience-dependent modification of internal structure, in a stimulus specific manner that alters the way the system will respond to a stimulus in the future as a function of its past. (Baluška and Levin, 2016: 902)

The fact that extracellular slime is a structure located outside of a plasmodium places its status as memory at odds with this characterisation of biological memory – a characterisation which seems to honour the internalist assumption common to traditional cognitive science and psychology that all cognitive processes occur inside the boundaries of an organism. There have been a number of arguments foisted against this assumption which I take to be compelling and thus I will not rehearse them here (see Clark and Chalmers, 1998; Sims and Kiverstein, 2022). It should be noted that this characterisation of biological memory is both phyletically neutral, *and* it rules out just any temporally contingent response (e.g., a broken bone) from counting as memory due to its emphasis on stimulus specificity (cf. Colaço, 2022). Moreover, this characterisation does not distinguish memory as a cognitive capacity from memory that is not. In fact, the process of experience-dependent structural modification referred to 'may or may not involve a degree of intelligence' (Baluška and Levin, 2016: 902).[38] One question that arises then is what distinguishes memory *qua* cognitive capacity from memory that is not?

Getting some purchase on this question is crucial for warranting a cognitive interpretation of extracellular slime and its use. Since Physarum's use of extracellular slime could represent a form of non-cognitive memory, Reid et al.'s claim that it is a kind of externalised spatial memory may be much less of a thorn in the side of traditional accounts of memory in cognitive science and

---

[38] Within the context of their article, Baluška and Levin (2016) do not distinguish cognition from intelligence. I will follow them here.

psychology, both of which focus upon investigating memory *qua cognitive capacity*. If this is the case, the task of distinguishing 'cognitive memory' from 'non-cognitive memory' becomes one of utmost importance.

Another telling feature of Baluška and Levin's characterisation of biological memory is the notion that structural modification is *experience-dependent*. Note that it is left open as to whether experience arises by way of learning or by some other means in which an environmental factor affects an organism's future behavioural tendencies. Moreover, if learning is taken to be a necessary condition for memory, it rules out viewing extracellular slime as memory (either cognitive or non-cognitive) because plasmodial secretion of extracellular slime is not a structural modification that results from learning.[39] Thus, an initial answer to one of the primary questions above is suggested by Baluška and Levin's definition: not all memory is the result of learning.

In the next section, I will propose one way of distinguishing cognitive memory from non-cognitive memory in biological systems that is based on the notion of metabolic individuality discussed in Section 4.[40] I will then turn to few examples that buttress the claim that memory needn't be the result of learning. This will put us in a better place to understand where Physarum's use of extracellular slime stands with respect to its status as a form of memory.

5.2 Why Cognitive Memory Arises at the Level of the Metabolic Individual

As suggested by Baluška and Levin, not all memory qualifies as a cognitive process and hence there are some forms of memory which fall out of the scope of cognitive explanations. I would now like to suggest that one thing that distinguishes memory as a cognitive capacity from other forms of biological memory is that the former is something that arises at the level of an integrated metabolic individual and only marginally at the level of the subsystems making up that metabolic individual.

Recall, from Section 4, that a metabolic individual is an entity that is made up of metabolically integrated parts that work together in the service of that individual's persistence despite the continuous turnover of matter. Metabolic individuality comes in degrees as measured by the presence of a system's own metabolic machinery, metabolic integration of parts, and autonomy of metabolic functioning.

---

[39] Whereas extracellular slime is considered to be a medium for information *storage*, the causal interaction between a plasmodium and extracellular slime has been argued to represent a form of *recall* or what has been called 'memory making' (Sims and Kiverstein, 2022).

[40] For my purposes in this section, the notion of metabolic individuality that I shall use will be indifferent to what was called the 'orthodox' view and the expanded view that was argued in Section 4 is required to make sense of fragmentation and fusion patterns.

Metabolic individuals can be, but needn't be reproducers (i.e., Darwinian individuals), thus allowing for some heterospecific symbiotic associations that do not reproduce as a unit to nonetheless qualify as delineable units of function. Relatedly, metabolic individuals can be nested; a highly metabolically integrated individual can be made up of other metabolic individuals; however, those at lower organisational level(s) give up some of their metabolic independence (i.e., autonomy) for the continued functioning of the individual at the higher level. Taking all of these core features into account, how might the notion of metabolic individuality hint at where cognitive explanations of memory might get the most purchase? If metabolic individuals are first and foremost persisters (Godfrey-Smith, 2013a), and such self-maintenance is the fundamental background against which all cognitive capacities might be thought to arise (Lyon et al., 2021; Sims, 2023), then it would seem that the kind of memory (learning and decision making for that matter) that warrants possible cognitive explanation *qua* cognitive process is that which arises at the level of a metabolic individual (cf. Keijzer, 2021).

This suggestion requires some refining however: although this rules out entities that are clearly not metabolic individuals such as genes, viruses, and genetic regulatory networks, because metabolic individuality is a matter of degree, an immediate challenge to this approach is that it requires drawing a non-arbitrary line between how much metabolic individuality is required to warrant memory being subject to cognitive explanation and how much is too little. Whilst I am sceptical that such a non-arbitrary line can be drawn, there is another way to decide upon the matter. It involves considering levels of biological organisation and their *relative degrees of metabolic individuality*. Even if some entity qualifies as a marginal metabolic individual, the fact that it is part of a larger system which has an even higher degree of metabolic individuality would suggest that the behaviour of the organisational level with the highest degree of relative metabolic individuality would be subject to explanation in terms of cognitive memory. To be clear, being subject to cognitive explanation means that the observed memory can be tested or investigated using criteria from specific theories of cognition (e.g., criteria for spatial memory, procedural memory, etc.). Satisfying those criteria, however, is an additional step, and one that can fail. On the other hand, if an entity fails to be a metabolic individual or fails to score as having the highest degree of relative metabolic individuality, investigating its observed memory using cognitive theories would constitute a category error.

Next, we will consider what this suggests about where the use of cognitive explanation of memory is warranted across different levels of biological organisation, beginning with bodily cells then and working up to groups of metabolic individuals. Two questions will be addressed at each level: (1) how is memory exhibited *and* (2) does the entity/entities occupying that specific level qualify as a metabolic individual?

5.3 Using Metabolic Individuality to Identify the Appropriate Level for Cognitive Explanations

5.3.1 Somatic Cells and Cellular Memory

In contrast to germ cells, somatic cells undergo differentiation during development, giving rise to various cell types that collectively form the tissues, organs, fibres, and bone structures of multicellular organisms. Each somatic cell of a specific type can produce daughter cells of the same type through the process of development and cell division (mitosis). While it is true that the genetic information encoded in the DNA of each cell contributes to the organism's overall structure, somatic cell differentiation relies on more than just the genetic code. This is where the concept of cellular memory earns its salt.

'Cellular memory' refers to the mechanisms that ensure the stability and preservation of specific characteristics and functions in differentiated cells as they go through mitosis (D'Urso and Brickner, 2014). These mechanisms often involve epigenetic modifications to gene function that are not the result of changes in DNA sequence (e.g., DNA methylation and histone modification) (Jablonka and Lamb, 2020). Cellular memory helps explain how a particular somatic cell type and its lineage maintain their unique identity during development and across cell division, allowing for the diversity and specialisation of cells in multicellular organisms. Is the cellular memory of somatic cells an example of cognitive memory? This depends, or so I would like to argue, on whether somatic cells are metabolic individuals (or have a high degree of metabolic individuality).

Somatic cells possess their own metabolic machinery and can perform basic metabolic processes independently *to a certain degree*, as demonstrated by their ability to be cultured in vitro. However, successful cultivation of somatic cells in a laboratory setting necessitates the creation of a controlled environment that replicates bodily conditions. In the natural bodily environment, the cooperation and metabolic interaction among different somatic cells and cell types are essential for each cell's physiological function. While somatic cells have their own metabolic machinery, their continued operation and viability rely heavily on constant metabolic integration with other cells and organs. For instance, a heart cell indirectly depends on cells in the stomach and small intestine to obtain metabolites from digested food, facilitated by the bloodstream. Thus, somatic cells, despite having their own metabolic machinery, are highly integrated into and metabolically dependent upon a larger metabolic system and cannot be considered bona fide metabolic individuals. This suggests that their cellular memory is not subject to cognitive explanation.

This conclusion is consistent with acknowledging that cellular memory can be fruitfully modelled 'as if' it was a cognitive process (cf. Pezzulo and Levin, 2016). However, due to the evolutionary path that somatic cells have followed, favouring the suppression of their metabolic independence in favour of the autonomy of the larger metabolic entity they constitute (such as the organism), treating them as cognitive agents, if I am correct, bottoms out as a useful fiction (e.g., helping to identify and highlight similar underlying mechanisms in use).

5.3.2 Immune Systems and Immunological Memory

The immune system is a complex network composed of cells, organs, and signalling molecules found in all multicellular organisms. Its primary role is to serve as a defence mechanism against various pathogens, such as harmful bacteria, viruses, and parasites. When these invaders are detected, the immune system deploys immune cells to eliminate them. To understand the concept of immunological memory, it is essential to consider the idea of 'affinity maturation'. This refers to the process by which certain immune cells, due to the specific conformation of their membrane receptors, have a stronger attraction to pathogens (Paul, 2003). In simpler terms, these immune cells have receptors that match the 3D shape of the antigens on the pathogen's surface. When these cells 'recognise' a pathogen, they release biochemical signals that are received by other immune cells. These signals convey information about the identity of the encountered pathogen, enabling the immune system to mount a targeted response.

Crucially, immune cells with a higher affinity for pathogens undergo more controlled mutation during cell division than those with lower affinity. As a result, over several generations of cell division, the immune cell line with higher pathogen affinity becomes even more specialised and effective. These immune cells have longer lifespans and form part of a repository known as 'immunological memory' (Farber et al., 2016). When an organism encounters the same pathogen in the future, the immune cells within the immunological memory can respond rapidly and effectively to eliminate the specific pathogens or any similar pathogens with antigens that share a similar protein conformation.

Is the immune system a metabolic individual and, more to the point, does it have a degree of metabolic individuality that is greater than that of the organism in which it is situated? I think the answer is a resounding no. Like other somatic cells, immune cells do have their own metabolic machinery and a certain degree of metabolic autonomy. That said, the long-term functioning of metabolic processes and persistence of the network of immune-specific cells and molecules that make up the immune system is dependent upon their being functionally integrated within an organism; the immune cells with high pathogen affinity that are maintained in the immune memory repertoire, for example, require energy and nutrients to function, which are supplied by various non-immune system cells and tissues. Relative to the organism that harbours immune cells, the continued functioning of their metabolic machinery is tied up with the encompassing organismal system within which the immune system has evolved to function as a part of. Therefore, like the cellular memory of somatic cells within a multicellular organism, immunological memory of the immune system, I would like to argue is not subject to cognitive explanation for the same reason.

5.3.3 Organisms and Organismal Memory

The vast majority of memory research in cognitive science and comparative psychology has been focused on metazoans such as humans, primates, rats, pigeons, corvids, sea slugs, and nematodes – paradigmatic organisms. Such research has investigated organismal memory using behavioural change to operationalise memory (Shettleworth, 2010), in addition to studying encoding, storage, and recall by way of identifying possible neuronal mechanisms (Gershman, 2023; Colaço and Najenson, 2023). Assuming that all organisms are metabolic individuals that exhibit a higher degree of metabolic individuality than their parts, and that explanations in terms of cognitive memory are warranted at the level of biological organisation where there is the highest relative degree of metabolic individuality, that organisms represent the paradigmatic biological level at which cognitive memory research has been investigated should come as no surprise. I shall assume the claim that organismal memory is indeed subject to explanation in terms of cognition and is therefore uncontroversial and spills no further ink on the matter here. There is, however, a question as to whether collections of organisms can exhibit an even higher relative degree of metabolic individuality than organisms.

5.3.4 Ant Colonies and Collective Memory

Eusocial insect societies, exemplified by certain ant, bee, and termite species, can be characterised as socially integrated colonies that involve multiple generations living together, cooperating in offspring care, and exhibiting a division of reproductive labour where non-reproductive 'workers' assist reproductive 'queens' (Wilson and Hölldobler, 2005). The idea that such societies can be viewed as biological individuals can be traced at least as far back as W. M. Wheeler's (1911) now-classic article 'The ant colony as an organism'. This idea has been developed since then with some biologists and philosophers viewing various eusocial colonies as 'superorganisms' (Willson and Sober, 1989). These are groups of individual organisms that exhibit behaviours only arising at the level of the collective (e.g., complex foraging patterns, colony defence, reproduction, etc.) (also see Gordon, 2010). This brings us to the questions of whether a eusocial ant colony can be seen as exhibiting memory at the level of the colony and, if so, whether such memory should receive treatment as a cognitive process? Let's take each of these questions in turn.

Research by biologist Deborah Gordon seems to support an affirmative answer to the first question. Using Harvester ants (*Pogonomyrmex barbatus*), Gordon (1989) conducted a series of disturbance experiments in which she strategically interfered with the various tasks of different workers. When toothpick obstacles were placed, it led workers to move them; when trails were blocked, foraging efforts on the part of foragers increased; when a disturbance was created it lead to attempts by patrollers to suppress those disturbances. While each experiment directly affected only one worker group, the behaviour of other groups of workers altered because the activity of workers allocated to one task is dependent upon the rate of brief encounters with workers doing other tasks (Gordon, 1989). Strikingly, after a few days of repeating the experiment, it was observed that the colonies maintained the altered behaviour (i.e., switching tasks and nest positions) in the absence of the disturbances and only gradually did the undisturbed task allocation patterns resume. The changing behaviour of the colony suggests that although individual ants may not retain any memory of the disturbance, a colony-level memory of the disturbance was formed (Gordon, 2018).

Is such colony-level memory the kind of memory that can be subject to cognitive explanation? Answering this question, if what I have been arguing is correct, involves evaluating whether the colony can be viewed as a metabolic individual and if it has a higher degree of metabolic individuality relative to the individual ants making up the colony *or* the system which the colony is a part of. Firstly, I think that an ant colony can be viewed as a metabolic individual for at least three reasons using the concept of metabolic individuality reviewed in Section 4: (1) a colony is made up of heterogeneous parts (i.e., ants with different – yet flexible – task allocations) that function together so as to maintain the colony despite turnover of individual parts (ants); (2) there is a high degree of cooperation and metabolic integration between those parts – something that is evidenced by Gordon's disturbance experiment; and (3) metabolic integration of parts – at least in some colonies – is underwritten by various attractant or repellent biochemical marks (e.g., pheromones signals) (Sumpter and Beekman, 2002), colony-level reciprocal food sharing in the form of 'trophallaxis' (i.e., the oral-oral and oral-anal exchange of nourishing fluids) (LeBoeuf, 2017), and rate of entering and exiting the nest (Gordon, 2010).

Assuming that there is no colony-containing biological system that scores higher than the colony in terms of metabolic individuality, the question to focus upon is whether a colony scores higher in terms of being a metabolic individual than an individual ant? I would like to argue that ants and colonies come close to having a similar score, close enough to regard memory in either of them as subject to cognitive explanation. This depends on whether an ant is functioning as a part of a colony or is isolated from the colony. When functioning in the colony, an ant 'surrenders' some of its metabolic independence for that of the colony. The nature of colony life is highly cooperative, such that the distribution of tasks (defence, nutritive, etc.) has viability benefits for most of the individual ants in the colony. Such dependence on the colony suggests that it has a higher score relative to an individual ant. Individual ants, however, have not evolved in such a way that their metabolic independence has become fully supressed for colony-level metabolic autonomy or cannot be regained to a degree if an ant finds itself isolated from its colony. Unlike somatic cells or an immune system, ants in a colony have not evolved within a spatial boundary. This spatial degree of freedom may allow individual ants to retain their independence as metabolic individuals while simultaneously allowing them to be part of a highly integrated metabolic superorganism, the task-allocation flexibility of which is dependent upon the ant parts maintaining their metabolic individuality and spatial degree of freedom.

Taking these points into account, I would like to suggest that both the colony-level memory and individual ant memory are subject to cognitive explanation. Importantly, this does not necessarily mean that they will conform to specific criteria demanded by various cognitive memory theories. Rather, it means that it is not a category error to apply such criteria to them. The determination of this matter is likely to hinge on careful examination of the broader task, such as navigation, in which memory is employed. This task may often involve learning, but sometimes not, as we shall now see.

5.4 Memory as a Result of Learning versus Memory as a Result of Inheritance

Learning may be understood broadly as a form of information processing that results in experience-dependent changes of behaviour as adapted to local environmental conditions (Dussutour, 2021). It includes, but is not limited to, processes like conditioning, habituation, sensitisation, and trial-and-error learning. Setting aside, momentarily, the question of whether the particular kinds of memory mentioned are subject to cognitive explanation, let us consider whether learning plays a part in each of them. Starting with cellular memory that constrains somatic cell differentiation through development and over mitosis: while early differentiating cells may learn in response to encountering epigenetic factors via their relative position to other cells, the memory possessed by cell progeny is not the result of learning; rather, it is the result of the progeny's inherited epigenetic marks that persist over mitosis. Immunological memory may be seen as a result of learning. Immune system cells detect pathogens and, due to affinity maturation and controlled mutation of cells with higher pathogen affinity, information regarding pathogens is stored and used to direct the system's future immune responses.

On some occasions organismal memory can be the result of learning. For example, conditioning, where repeatedly encountering stimulus–stimulus pairs separated by a time interval across a training period, is representative of the kind of cognitive psychology textbook understanding of how memory is formed. On other occasions organismal memory can be the result of inheritance without learning. This is clear in cases of say memory transfer where memory has been experimentally induced via 'artificial inheritance'. For instance, *Physarum* plasmodia that have been repeatedly exposed to a non-lethal amount of an aversive stimulus learn to ignore it and, thus, become habituated to the specific stimulus.[41] It was shown that when a habituated plasmodium fuses with a plasmodium that has not been habituated, the larger post-fusion cell responds in a habituated manner (Vogel and Dussutour, 2016). Similarly, memory transfer has been shown to occur with 'sensitisation' or a decrease in response threshold based on prior experience. RNA taken from a trained *Aplysia californica* (a kind of giant sea slug) that learned to respond to shock with a longer siphon withdraw reflex when injected into an untrained *Aplysia* resulted in the naïve *Aplysia* responding to the shock in the same sensitised manner (Bédécarrats et al., 2018). In each of these cases memory directs behaviour without learning having occurred in the transferee.

Lastly, what about ant colony memory? In the case previously described, memory of the colony seems to result from learning at the level of the colony. Such learning and memory are underwritten by 'interaction dynamics' (i.e., the rate of interaction and rate of response) between various ants performing different tasks in the colony (Gordon, 2010). Such interaction dynamics can include not only interaction with other ants but also interaction with environment-mediated signals (pheromone trails) left by ants that iteratively affect the nature of such dynamics (Sumpter and Beekman, 2002). All of this is compatible with the fact that individual ants can learn and direct their navigational behaviour according to

---

[41] More precisely, habituation occurs when there is a decrease in response to a specific cue to repeated encounters with that stimulus.

visual cues in the environment (Aron et al., 1993). Such learning may contribute to colony-level memory that can remain stable for many years, 'outliving' the individual ants that contributed to the formation and stabilisation of the colony memory (see Rosengren and Fortelius, 1987).

5.5 A Fourfold Analysis of Biological Memory

Using the results of the analyses in Sections 5.3 and 5.4, there are four possible categories of memory which are thrown into relief: *memory subject to cognitive explanation, memory that is not subject to cognitive explanation, memory that results from learning,* and *memory that does not result from learning.* These opposing memory category pairs can be situated along two dimensions, illustrating how they interact within a fourfold analysis of biological memory (Table 3). There are some cases that are more clearly subject to cognitive explanation than others. Making a decision regarding the latter cases will likely depend upon how memory is used in the wider context of a particular task and hence satisfying the criteria for the specific form of memory (e.g., spatial memory, etc.) being investigated.

Returning to the cognitive interpretation of Reid et al.'s experiment: if what I have argued here is correct, given that a Physarum plasmodium scores higher with respective to metabolic individuality than its parts (e.g., nuclei) or higher than any other biological system which it is a part of, it follows that a plasmodium's use of extracellular slime as it navigates across complex environments falls into the category of memory that is subject to cognitive explanation and that is not the result of learning. Such memory represents a paradigm example of external niche construction (ENC) (Section 2).

6 Conclusion

Philosophy of biology brims with a panoply of interesting and difficult puzzles, challenging much of our quotidian understanding of the biological world. This Element has served as a starting point and a full-bodied exercise in illustrating how attention to the outlier model organism – the acellular slime mould, *P. polycephalum* – can go a long way in terms of bringing some of those puzzles to the fore; a long way in providing concrete cases with which to consider just how wondrous and wondrously unintuitive the biological world can be. Given that biological theory is not an island that is somehow isolated from our pre-theoretical assumptions, the work that Physarum can do does not stop at challenging folk biological assumptions. This Element represents a mere scratching of the perennial surface when it comes to how Physarum can contribute to the philosophy of biology. If it has piqued the interest of the

Table 3 A fourfold analysis of memory and some examples

	Memory subject to cognitive explanation	Memory not subject to cognitive explanation
Memory that results from learning	**Cases of trial-and -error learning, habituation and conditioning at the level of the organism** (e.g., habituation in *P. polycephalum* (Vogel and Dussutour, 2016); habituation in *Stentor coeruleus* (Rajan et al., 2023); trial-and-error learning in *Stentor roeseli* (Jennings, 1902; Dexter et al., 2019); conditioning in *Paramecium aurelia* (Gelber, 1962; Armus et al., 2006); conditioning in *Amoeba proteus* (de la Fuente et al., 2019); conditioning in *Caenorhabditis elegans* (Morrison et al.,1999); and conditioning in dogs (Pavlov, [1897] 1902)) **Some cases of learning at the level of the colony or 'superorganism'** (e.g., learned task reallocation in response to perturbation (Gordon et al., 1989))	**Associative conditioning at levels below the metabolic individual** (e.g., conditioning in gene regulatory networks (Biswas et al., 2021)) **Conditioning at levels below the highest scoring metabolic individual** (e.g., associative learning in purkinje cells (Jirenhed et al., 2017)) **Immunological memory** (e.g., primed antibody response to pathogens at level of immune system (Cohen, 1992)) **Some cases of learning at the level of the colony or 'superorganism'** (?)
Memory that does not result from learning	**Transferred memory that results in matching behavioural profile in transferee to that of the trained individual that learned** (e.g., Physarum fusion habituation transfer (Vogel and Dussutour, 2016); sensitisation transfer in Aplysia (Bédécarrats et al., 2018)) **Production and use of environmentally mediated cues and signals for spatial navigation** (e.g., Physarum's production and use of extracellular slime to navigate complex environments (Reid et al., 2012, 2013))	**Epigenetically stabilised somatic cell differentiation and development** (e.g., epigenetic regulation in pluripotent stem cells (Watanabe et al., 2013)) **Transgenerational cellular memory** (e.g., proliferation and maintenance of heterogeneity in bacterial cell characteristics over multiple generations due to epigenetically inherited marks (Vashistha et al., 2021))

philosopher to look further into the fascinating life cycle and behaviour of slime mould, if it has inspired the biologist to consider the deep philosophical challenges made salient by Physarum, or if it has provided some common ground for future research that both the philosopher and the biologist can tread upon in tandem, then 'Slime Mould and Philosophy' has done its job.

References

Aaby, Bendik Hellem, and Grant Ramsey. 2019. 'Three Kinds of Niche Construction'. *The British Journal for the Philosophy of Science* 73 (2): 351–72.

Armus, Harvard L., Amber R. Montgomery, and Rebecca L. Gurney. 2006. 'Discrimination Learning and Extinction in Paramecia (*P. Caudatum*)'. *Psychological Reports* 98 (3): 705–11.

Aron, Serge, R. Beckers, Jean-Louis Deneubourg, and Jacques Pasteels. 1993. 'Memory and Chemical Communication in the Orientation of Two Mass-Recruiting Ant Species'. *Insectes Sociaux* 40 (4): 369–80.

Bédécarrats, Alexis, Shanping Chen, Kaycey Pearce, Diancai Cai, and David L. Glanzman. 2018. 'RNA from Trained Aplysia Can Induce an Epigenetic Engram for Long-Term Sensitization in Untrained Aplysia'. *Eneuro* 5 (3): ENEURO.0038–18.2018: 1–11.

Baedke, Jan, Alejandro Fábregas-Tejeda, and Guido I. Prieto. 2021. 'Unknotting Reciprocal Causation between Organism and Environment'. *Biology and Philosophy* 36: 48.

Bailey, Juliet. 1997. 'Building a Plasmodium: Development in the Acellular Slime Mould Physarum Polycephalum'. *BioEssays* 19 (11): 985–92.

Baluška, František, and Michael Levin. 2016. 'On Having No Head: Cognition throughout Biological Systems'. *Frontiers in Psychology* 7 (June): 902.

Bateson, Patrick, and Peter Gluckman. 2011. *Plasticity, Robustness, Development and Evolution*. Cambridge: Cambridge University Press.

Biswas, Surama, Santosh Manicka, Erik Hoel, and Michael Levin. 2021. 'Gene Regulatory Networks Exhibit Several Kinds of Memory: Quantification of Memory in Biological and Random Transcriptional Networks'. *IScience* (February): 102131.

Bitbol, Michel, and Pier Luigi Luisi. 2004. 'Autopoiesis with or without Cognition: Defining Life at Its Edge'. *Journal of the Royal Society Interface* 1 (1): 99–107.

Blackwell, Meredith. 1984. 'Myxomycetes and Their Arthropod Associates'. In *Fungus–Insect Relationships: Perspectives in Ecology and Evolution*, (Eds.) Quentin D. Wheeler and Meredith Blackwell. pp. 67–90. New York: Columbia University Press.

Bock, Walter J. 1980. 'The Definition and Recognition of Biological Adaptation'. *Integrative and Comparative Biology* 20 (1): 217–27.

Bodnar, Andrea G. 2014. 'Cellular and Molecular Mechanisms of Negligible Senescence: Insight from the Sea Urchin'. *Invertebrate Reproduction & Development* 59 (sup1): 23–27.

Briard, Léa, Cécile Goujarde, Christopher Bousquet, and Audrey Dussutour. 2020. 'Stress Signalling in Acellular Slime Moulds and Its Detection by Conspecifics'. *Philosophical Transactions of the Royal Society B: Biological Sciences* 375 (1802): 20190470.

Cano, Raúl J., and Monica K. Borucki. 1995. 'Revival and Identification of Bacterial Spores in 25- to 40-Million-Year-Old Dominican Amber'. *Science (New York, N.Y.)* 268 (5213): 1060–64.

Chiu, Lynn. 2019. 'Decoupling, Commingling, and the Evolutionary Significance of Experiential Niche Construction'. In *Evolutionary Causation: Biological and Philosophical Reflections*, (Eds.) Tobias Oller and Kevin N. Laland. pp. 299–322. Cambridge: MIT Press.

Clark, Andy, and David Chalmers. 1998. 'The Extended Mind'. *Analysis* 58 (1): 7–19.

Clark, Jim, and Edward F. Haskins. 2012. 'Plasmodial Incompatibility in the Myxomycetes: A Review'. *Mycosphere* 3 (2): 131–41.

Clark, Jim, and Edward F. Haskins. 2016. 'Myxomycete Plasmodial Biology: A Review'. *Mycosphere* 6 (6): 643–58.

Clarke, Ellen. 2010. 'The Problem of Biological Individuality'. *Biological Theory* 5 (4): 312–25.

Clegg, James S. 1979. 'Metabolism and Intercellular Environment: The Viciml-Water Network Model'. In *Cell Associated Water*, (Eds.) W. Drost-Hansen and J. S. Clegg, pp. 363–413. New York: Academic Press.

Clegg, James S. 1986. 'The Physical Properties and Metabolic States of Artemia Cysts at Low Water Contents: The 'Water Replacement Hypothesis'. In *Membranes, Metabolism and Dry Organisms*, (Ed.) A. C. Leopold, pp. 169–87. New York: Cornell University Press.

Clegg, James S. 2001. 'Cryptobiosis: A Peculiar State of Biological Organization'. *Comparative Biochemistry and Physiology. Part B, Biochemistry & Molecular Biology* 128 (4): 613–24.

Cleland, Carol. 2019. *The Quest for a Universal Theory of Life: Searching for Life as We Don't Know It*. Cambridge: Cambridge University Press.

Clements, Frederic E. 1916. *Plant Succession: An Analysis of the Development of Vegetation*. Washington: Carnegie Institution of Washington.

Cohen, Irun R. 1992. 'The Cognitive Paradigm and the Immunological Homunculus'. *Immunology Today* 13 (12): 490–94.

Colaço, David. 2022. 'What Counts as a Memory? Definitions, Hypotheses, and 'Kinding in Progress'. *Philosophy of Science* 89 (1): 89–106.

Colaço, David, and Jonathan Najenson. 2023. 'Where Memory Resides: Is There a Rivalry between Molecular and Synaptic Models of Memory?' *Philosophy of Science* (October): 1–11.

Collins, O'Neil Ray. 1979. 'Myxomycete Biosystematics: Some Recent Developments and Future Research Opportunities'. *The Botanical Review* 45 (2): 145–201.

Darwin, Charles. 1839/1967. *The Voyage of the Beagle*. New York: Dent.

Darwin, Charles. 1881. *The Formation of Vegetable Mould through the Action of Worm, with Observations on Their Habits*. London: John Murray.

de la Fuente, Ildefonso M., Carlos Bringas, Iker Malaina, et al. 2019. 'Evidence of Conditioned Behavior in Amoebae'. *Nature Communications* 10: 3690.

Dexter, Joseph P., Sudhakaran Prabakaran, and Jeremy Gunawardena. 2019. 'A Complex Hierarchy of Avoidance Behaviors in a Single-Cell Eukaryote'. *Current Biology* 29 (24): 4323–29.

Dupré, John, and Maureen A. O'Malley. 2009. 'Varieties of Living Things: Life at the Intersection of Lineage and Metabolism'. *Philosophy and Theory in Biology* 1: 20170609.

D'Urso, Agustina, and Jason H. Brickner. 2014. 'Mechanisms of Epigenetic Memory'. *Trends in Genetics: TIG* 30 (6): 230–36.

Dussutour, Audrey. 2021. 'Learning in Single Cell Organisms'. *Biochemical and Biophysical Research Communications* 564: 92–102.

Dussutour, Audrey, Tanya Latty, Madeleine Beekman, and Stephen J. Simpson. 2010. 'Amoeboid Organism Solves Complex Nutritional Challenges'. *Proceedings of the National Academy of Sciences of the United States of America* 107 (10): 4607–11.

Epstein, Leo, Zeth Dubois, Jessica Smith, Yunha Lee, and Kyle Harrington. 2021. 'Complex Population Dynamics in a Spatial Microbial Ecosystem with Physarum Polycephalum'. *Biosystems* 208 (October): 104483.

Ereshefsky, Marc, and Makmiller Pedroso. 2015. 'Rethinking Evolutionary Individuality'. *Proceedings of the National Academy of Sciences* 112 (33): 10126–32.

Farber, Donna L., Mihai G. Netea, Andreas Radbruch, Klaus Rajewsky, and Rolf M. Zinkernagel. 2016. 'Immunological Memory: Lessons from the Past and a Look to the Future'. *Nature Reviews Immunology* 16 (2): 124–28.

Fusco, Giuseppe, and Alessandro Minelli. 2019. *The Biology of Reproduction*. Cambridge: Cambridge University Press.

Gánti, Tibor. 1970/2003. *The Principles of Life*. New York: Oxford University Press.

Gelber, Beatrice. 1957. 'Food or Training in *Paramecium*?' *Science* 126 (3287): 1340–41.

Gershman, Samuel J. 2023. 'The Molecular Memory Code and Synaptic Plasticity: A Synthesis'. *Biosystems* 224 (February): 104825.

Gilbert, Scott F. 2000. *Developmental Biology*, 6th ed. Sunderland: Sinauer Associates.

Gilbert, Jack A., Martin J. Blaser, J. Gregory Caporaso, et al. 2018. 'Current Understanding of the Human Microbiome'. *Nature Medicine* 24 (4): 392–400.

Godfrey-Smith, Peter. 1996. *Complexity and the Function of Mind in Nature*. Cambridge: Cambridge University Press.

Godfrey-Smith, Peter. 2001. Environmental Complexity and the Evolution of Cognition. In *The Evolution of Intelligence*, (Eds.) R. J. Sternberg and J. C. Kaufman (pp. 223–49). Mahwah: Lawenece Erlbaum Associates.

Godfrey-Smith, Peter. 2009. *Darwinian Populations and Natural Selection*. New York: Oxford University Press.

Godfrey-Smith, Peter. 2013a. 'Darwinian Individuals'. In *From Groups to Individuals: Perspectives on Biological Associations and Emerging Individuality*, (Eds.) F. Bouchard and P. Huneman, pp. 17–36. Cambridge: MIT Press.

Godfrey-Smith, Peter. 2013b. *Philosophy of Biology*. Princeton: Princeton University Press.

Godfrey-Smith, Peter. 2016. 'Complex Life Cycles and the Evolutionary Process'. *Philosophy of Science* 83 (5): 816–27.

Gordon, Deborah M. 1989. 'Dynamics of Task Switching in Harvester Ants'. *Animal Behaviour* 38 (2): 194–204.

Gordon, Deborah M. 2010. *Ant Encounters: Interaction Networks and Colony Behavior*. Princeton: Princeton University Press.

Gordon, Deborah M. 2018. An Ant Colony Has Memories That Its Individual Members Don't Have. *Aeon*.

Gorman, Jessica A., and Adam S. Wilkins. 1980. 'VI. Developmental Phases in the Life Cycle of Physarum and Related Myxomycetes'. In *Growth and Differentiation in Physarum Polycephalum*, (Eds.) William F. Dove and Harold P. Rusch. pp. 157–201. Princeton: Princeton University Press.

Gray, William D. 1945. 'The Existence of Physiological Strains in Physarum Polycephalum'. *American Journal of Botany* 32 (3): 157–60.

Herron, Matthew D. 2017. 'Cells, Colonies, and Clones: Individuality in the Volvocine Algae'. In *Biological Individuality: Integrating Scientific, Philosophical, and Historical Perspectives*, (Eds.) Scott Lidgard and Lynn K. Nyhart, pp. 318–48. Chicago: University of Chicago Press.

Hinton, Howard E. 1960. 'Cryptobiosis in the Larva of *Polypedilum Vanderplanki Hint.* (Chironomidae)'. *Journal of Insect Physiology* 5 (3–4): 286–300.

Huxley, Thomas. 1859/2008. *The Oceanic Hydrozoa: A Description of the Calycophoridae and Physophoridae Observed during the Voyage of H. M. S. Rattlesnake in the Years 18*. Exeter: Edward Bowditch.

Huxley, Julian. 1912/2022. *The Individual in the Animal Kingdom*. Cambridge: MIT Press.

Jablonka, Eva, and Marion Lamb. 2020. *Inheritance Systems and the Extended Synthesis*. Cambridge: Cambridge University Press.

Janzen, Daniel H. 1977. 'What Are Dandelions and Aphids?' *The American Naturalist* 111 (979): 586–89.

Jennings, Herbert S. (1902). 'Studies on Reactions to Stimuli in Unicellular Organisms IX—On the Behavior of Fixed Infusoria (Stentor and Vorticella) with Special Reference to the Modifiability of Protozoan Reactions'. *American Journal of Physiol*ogy 8: 23–60.

Jirenhed, Dan-Anders, Anders Rasmussen, Fredrik Johansson, and Germund Hesslow. 2017. 'Learned Response Sequences in Cerebellar Purkinje Cells'. *Proceedings of the National Academy of Sciences* 114 (23): 6127–32.

Keijzer, Fred. 2021. 'Demarcating Cognition: The Cognitive Life Sciences'. *Synthese* 198 (1): 137–57.

Keilin, David. 1959. 'The Leeuwenhoek Lecture – the Problem of Anabiosis or Latent Life: History and Current Concept'. *Proceedings of the Royal Society of London. Series B – Biological Sciences* 150 (939): 149–91.

Keller, Harold W., Courtney M. Kilgore, Sydney E. Everhart, et al. 2008. 'Myxomycete Plasmodia and Fruiting Bodies: Unusual Occurrences and User-Friendly Study Techniques', January.

Kessler, Daniel. 1982. 'Plasmodial Structure and Motility'. In *Cell Biology of Physarum and Didymium*, Vol. 1. (Eds.) H. C. Aldrich and J. W. Daniel, pp. 145–208. New York: Academic Press.

Laland, Kevin N., John Odling-Smee, and Marcus W. Feldman. 2000. 'Niche Construction, Biological Evolution, and Cultural Change'. *Behavioral and Brain Sciences* 23 (1): 131–46.

Lane, Nick. 2016. *The Vital Question*. London: Profile Books.

Latty, Tanya, and Madeleine Beekman. 2010. 'Food Quality and the Risk of Light Exposure Affect Patch-Choice Decisions in the Slime Mold Physarum Polycephalum'. *Ecology* 91 (1): 22–27.

Latty, Tanya, and Madeleine Beekman. 2011. 'Irrational Decision-Making in an Amoeboid Organism: Transitivity and Context-Dependent Preferences'. *Proceedings of the Royal Society B: Biological Sciences* 278 (1703): 307–12.

LeBoeuf, Adria C. 2017. 'Trophallaxis'. *Current Biology* 27 (24): R1299–R1300.

Levin, Michael. 2019. 'The Computational Boundary of a 'Self': Developmental Bioelectricity Drives Multicellularity and Scale-Free Cognition'. *Frontiers in Psychology* 10: 2688

Lewontin, Richard C. 1983. 'The Organism as the Subject and Object of Evolution'. *Scientia* 77 (18): 63–82.

Lewontin, Richard C. 1985. 'Adaptation'. In *The Dialectical Biologist*, (Eds.) R. Levins and R. C. Lewontin, pp. 65–84. Cambridge: Harvard University Press.

Levis, Nicholas A., and David W. Pfennig. 2016. 'Evaluating 'Plasticity-First' Evolution in Nature: Key Criteria and Empirical Approaches'. *Trends in Ecology & Evolution* 31 (7): 563–74. https://doi.org/10.1016/j.tree.2016.03.012.

Lidgard, Scott, and Lynn K. Nyhart. 2017. *Biological Individuality Integrating Scientific, Philosophical, and Historical Perspectives*. Chicago: The University of Chicago Press.

Love, Alan C., and Brigandt, Ingo. 2017. 'Philosophical Dimensions of Individuality'. In *Biological Individuality: Integrating Scientific, Philosophical, and Historical Perspectives*, (Eds.) Scott Lidgard and Lynn K. Nyhart, pp. 318–48. Chicago: University of Chicago Press.

Lyon, Pamela, Fred Keijzer, Detlev Arendt, and Michael Levin. 2021. 'Reframing Cognition: Getting Down to Biological Basics'. *Philosophical Transactions of the Royal Society B: Biological Sciences* 376 (1820): 20190750.

Martin, William F., Sriram Garg, and Verena Zimorski. 2015. 'Endosymbiotic Theories for Eukaryote Origin'. *Philosophical Transactions of the Royal Society B: Biological Sciences* 370 (1678): 20140330.

Maturana, Humberto Romecin, and Francisco J. Varela. 1980. *Autopoiesis and Cognition: The Realization of the Living. With a Pref. To Autopoiesis by Sir Stafford Beer*. Dordrecht: D. Reidel.

Maynard Smith, John and Eörs Szathmáry. 2010. *The Major Transitions in Evolution*. Oxford: Oxford University Press.

McFall-Ngai, Margaret. 2014. 'Divining the Essence of Symbiosis: Insights from the Squid-Vibrio Model'. *PLoS Biology* 12 (2): e1001783.

Meincke, Anne Sophie, and John Dupré. 2020. *Biological Identity*. New York: Routledge.

Møbjerg, Nadja, and Ricardo Cardoso Neves. 2021. 'New Insights into Survival Strategies of Tardigrades'. *Comparative Biochemistry and Physiology Part A: Molecular & Integrative Physiology* 254 (April): 110890.

Morrison, Glenn E., Joseph Y. M. Wen, Susan Runciman, and Derek van der Kooy. 1999. 'Olfactory Associative Learning in Caenorhabditis Elegans Is

Impaired in Lrn-1 and Lrn-2 Mutants'. *Behavioral Neuroscience* 113 (2): 358–67.

Nakagaki, Toshiyuki. 2004. 'Smart Network Solutions in an Amoeboid Organism'. *Biophysical Chemistry* 107 (1): 1–5.

Nakagaki, Toshiyuki, Hiroyasu Yamada, and Ágota Tóth. 2000. 'Maze-Solving by an Amoeboid Organism.' *Nature* 407 (6803): 470–70.

Nakagaki, Toshiyuki, Hiroyasu Yamada, and Ágota Tóth. 2001. 'Path Finding by Tube Morphogenesis in an Amoeboid Organism'. *Biophysical Chemistry* 92 (1–2): 47–52.

Nakagaki, Toshiyuki, Ryo Kobayashi, Yasumasa Nishiura, and Tetsuo Ueda. 2004. 'Obtaining Multiple Separate Food Sources: Behavioural Intelligence in the Physarum Plasmodium'. *Proceedings of the Royal Society B: Biological Sciences* 271 (1554): 2305–10.

Odling-Smee, John F., Kevin N. Laland, and Marcus W. Feldman. 2003. *Niche Construction: The Neglected Process in Evolution.* Princeton: Princeton University Press.

Pagh, Kathryn I., and Mark R. Adelman. 1988. 'Video Supplement Assembly, Disassembly, and Movements of the Microfilament-Rich Ridge during the Amoeboflagellate Transformation In Physarum Polycephalum'. *Cytoskeleton* 11 (4): 223–34.

Patino-Ramirez, Fernando, Aurèle Boussard, Chloé Arson, and Audrey Dussutour. 2019. 'Substrate Composition Directs Slime Molds Behavior'. *Scientific Reports* 9 (1).

Paul, William. E. 2003. *Fundamental Immunology.* Philadelphia: Lippincott Williams & Wilkins.

Pavlov, Ivan P. 1897/1902. *The Work of the Digestive Glands.* London: Griffin.

Pezzulo, Giovanni, and Michael Levin. 2016. 'Top-down Models in Biology: Explanation and Control of Complex Living Systems above the Molecular Level'. *Journal of the Royal Society Interface* 13 (124): 20160555.

Pradeu, Thomas. 2016. 'Organisms or Biological Individuals? Combining Physiological and Evolutionary Individuality'. *Biology & Philosophy* 31 (6): 797–817.

Pradeu, Thomas, Mael Lemoine, Mahdi Khelfaoui, and Yves Gingras. 2021. 'Philosophy in Science: Can Philosophers of Science Permeate through Science and Produce Scientific Knowledge?' *The British Journal for the Philosophy of Science* 75(2): 375–416.

Queller, David C., and Joan E. Strassmann. 2009. 'Beyond Society: The Evolution of Organismality'. *Philosophical Transactions of the Royal Society B: Biological Sciences* 364 (1533): 3143–55.

Rajan, Deepa, Peter Chudinov, and Wallace Marshall. 2023. 'Studying Habituation in Stentor Coeruleus'. *JoVE (Journal of Visualized Experiments)*, 191 (January): e64692. https://doi.org/10.3791/64692.

Reid, Chris R. 2023. 'Thoughts from the Forest Floor: A Review of Cognition in the Slime Mould Physarum Polycephalum'. *Animal Cognition* 26: 1783–97.

Reid, Chris R., Tanya Latty, Audrey Dussutour, and Madeleine Beekman. 2012. 'Slime Mold Uses an Externalized Spatial 'Memory' to Navigate in Complex Environments'. *Proceedings of the National Academy of Sciences of the United States of America* 109 (43):17490–94.

Reid, Chris R., Madeleine Beekman, Tanya Latty, and Audrey Dussutour. 2013. 'Amoeboid Organism Uses Extracellular Secretions to Make Smart Foraging Decisions'. *Behavioral Ecology* 24 (4): 812–18.

Rikkinen, Jouko, David A. Grimaldi, and Alexander R. Schmidt. 2019. 'Morphological Stasis in the First Myxomycete from the Mesozoic, and the Likely Role of Cryptobiosis'. *Scientific Reports* 9 (1): 1–8.

Rosengren, Rainer, and Wilhelm Fortelius. 1987. 'Trail Communication and Directional Recruitment to Food in Red Wood Ants (Formica)'. *Annales Zoologici Fennici* 24 (2): 137–46.

Sagan, Lynn. 1967. 'On the Origin of Mitosing Cells'. *Journal of Theoretical Biology* 14 (3): 225–IN6.

Sagan, Carl. 2010. 'Definitions of life'. In *The Nature of Life: Classical and Contemporary Perspectives from Philosophy and Science*, M. Bedau & C. Cleland (Authors), pp. 303–306. Cambridge: Cambridge University Press.

Saigusa, Tetsu, Atsushi Tero, Toshiyuki Nakagaki, and Yoshiki Kuramoto. 2008. 'Amoebae Anticipate Periodic Events'. *Physical Review Letters* 100 (1): 1–5.

Sauer, Herbert W., Kenneth L. Babcock, and Harold P. Rusch. 1969. 'Sporulation in Physarum Polycephalum: A Model System for Studies on Differentiation'. *Experimental Cell Research* 57 (2): 319–27.

Schrödinger, Edward. 1944. *What Is Life?* Cambridge: Cambridge University Press.

Scott-Phillips, Thomas C., Kevin N. Laland, David M. Shuker, Thomas E. Dickins, and Stuart A. West. 2014. 'The Niche Construction Perspective: A Critical Appraisal'. *Evolution* 68 (5): 1231–43.

Seeley, Thomas D. 1989. 'The Honey Bee Colony as a Superorganism'. *American Scientist* 77 (6): 546–53.

Segev, Einat, Yoav Smith, and Sigal Ben-Yehuda. 2012. 'RNA Dynamics in Aging Bacterial Spores'. *Cell* 148 (1–2): 139–49.

Shatilovich, Anastasia, Vamshidhar R. Gade, Martin Pippel, et al. 2023. 'A Novel Nematode Species from the Siberian Permafrost Shares Adaptive

Mechanisms for Cryptobiotic Survival with C. Elegans Dauer Larva'. *PLOS Genetics* 19 (7): e1010798–98.

Sims, Matthew. 2023. 'The Principle of Dynamic Holism: Guiding Methodology for Investigating Cognition in Non-Neuronal Organisms'. *Philosophy of Science* 91 (2): 430–48.

Shettleworth, Sarah J. 2010. *Cognition, Evolution, and Behavior*, 2nd ed. New York: Oxford University Press.

Sims, Matthew, and Julian Kiverstein. 2022. 'Externalized Memory in Slime Mould and the Extended (Non-Neuronal) Mind'. *Cognitive Systems Research* 73 (June): 26–35.

Smith, David L., and Peter Robinson. 1975. 'The Effects of Spore Age on Germination and Gametophyte Development in Polypodium Vulgare L.' *New Phytologist* 74 (1): 101–108.

Smith-Ferguson, Jules, and Madeleine Beekman. 2019. 'Can't See the Colony for the Bees: Behavioural Perspectives of Biological Individuality'. *Biological Reviews* 94: 1935–46.

Smith-Ferguson, Jules, Chris R. Reid, Tanya Latty, and Madeleine Beekman. 2017. 'Hänsel, Gretel and the Slime Mould – How an External Spatial Memory Aids Navigation in Complex Environments'. *Journal of Physics D: Applied Physics* 50 (41): 414003.

Sperry, Megan, M., Nirosha J., Murugan, and Michael Levin. 2022. Studying Protista WBR and Repair Using *Physarum polycephalum*. In *Whole-Body Regeneration: Methods in Molecular Biology*, Vol. 2450, (Eds.) S. Blanchoud and B. Galliot, pp. 51–67. New York: Humana

Sterelny, Kim. 2003. *Thought in a Hostile World: The Evolution of Human Cognition*. Oxford: Blackwell.

Stephenson, Steven L., and Henry Stempen. 1994. *Myxomycetes*. Oregon: Timber Press.

Sugiura, Shinji, Yu Fukasawa, Ryo Ogawa, Shin-Ichi Kawakami, and Kazuo Yamazaki. 2019. 'Cross-Kingdom Interactions between Slime Molds and Arthropods: A Spore Dispersal Mutualism Hypothesis'. *Ecology* 100 (8).

Sultan, Sonia E. 2015. *Organism and Environment: Ecological Development, Niche Construction, and Adaptation*. Oxford: Oxford University Press.

Sumpter, David J. T, and Madeleine Beekman. 2002. 'From Nonlinearity to Optimality: Pheromone Trail Foraging by Ants'. *Animal Behaviour* 66 (2): 273–80.

Trappes, Rose, Behzad Nematipour, Marie I. Kaiser, et al. 2022. 'How Individualized Niches Arise: Defining Mechanisms of Niche Construction, Niche Choice, and Niche Conformance'. *BioScience* 72 (6): 538–48.

Varela, Francisco J. 1994. 'On Defining Life'. In *Self-Production of Supramolecular Structures*. NATO ASI Series, Vol. 446, (Eds.) G. R. Fleischaker, S. Colonna, and P. L. Luisi, pp. 23–31. Dordrecht: Springer.

Vashistha, Harsh, Maryam Kohram, and Hanna Salman. 2021. 'Non-Genetic Inheritance Restraint of Cell-to-Cell Variation'. *ELife* 10 (February): 1–16.

Vogel, David, Stamatios C. Nicolis, Alfonso Pérez-Escudero, et al. 2015. 'Phenotypic Variability in Unicellular Organisms: From Calcium Signalling to Social Behaviour'. *Proceedings of the Royal Society B: Biological Sciences* 282 (1819): 20152322–22.

Vogel, David, and Audrey Dussutour. 2016. 'Direct Transfer of Learned Behaviour via Cell Fusion in Non-neural Organisms'. *Proceedings of the Royal Society B: Biological Sciences* 283 (1845): 20162382.

Waddington, Conrad. 1969. 'Paradigm for an Evolutionary Process'. In *Towards a Theoretical Biology*, (Ed.) Conrad Hal Waddington, pp. 106–23. Edinburgh: Edinburgh University Press.

Watanabe, Akira, Yasuhiro Yamada, and Shinya Yamanaka. 2013. 'Epigenetic Regulation in Pluripotent Stem Cells: A Key to Breaking the Epigenetic Barrier'. *Philosophical Transactions of the Royal Society B: Biological Sciences* 368 (1609): 20120292.

West-Eberhard, Mary J. 2003. *Developmental Plasticity and Evolution*. Oxford: Oxford University Press.

Wharton, David A. 2003. *Life at the Limits: Organisms in Extreme Environments*. Cambridge: Cambridge University Press.

Wheeler, William Morton. 1911. 'The Ant-Colony as an Organism'. *Journal of Morphology* 22 (2): 307–25.

Wilson, Jessica. 2023. 'Determinables and Determinates'. *The Stanford Encyclopedia of Philosophy*, Edward N. Zalta and Uri Nodelman (Eds.) https://plato.stanford.edu/archives/spr2023/entries/determinate-determinables/.

Wilson, David Sloan, and Elliott Sober. 1989. 'Reviving the Superorganism'. *Journal of Theoretical Biology* 136 (3): 337–56.

Wilson, Edward O., and B. Holldobler. 2005. 'Eusociality: Origin and Consequences'. *Proceedings of the National Academy of Sciences* 102 (38): 13367–71.

Acknowledgements

I would like to thank the following people for the many discussions that shaped this Element and for providing comments on either all or parts of the manuscript: Jan Baedke, Nick Brancazio, David Colaço, Si Qiao Ding, John Dupré, Audrey Dussutour, Carrie Figdor, Debora Gordon, Jeremy Gunawardena, Eva Jablonka, Fred Keijzer, Michael Levin, Pamela Lyon, Kevin Mitchell, Kathryn Nave, Emma Otterski, Guido I. Prieto, Sofiia Rappe, Chris Reid, Tobias Schlict, Caroline Stankozi, Tobias Starzak, Stephen Stevenson, and Alejandro Fárbregas Tejeda. A very special thanks to two anonymous reviewers for their helpful comments and to Grant Ramsey and Michael Ruse for their support and encouragement to write this Element. Lastly, I am grateful to Benjamin Little for his unwavering love and being a constant source of inspiration. This research was made possible through generous support from the VolkswagenStiftung.

Cambridge Elements ☰

Philosophy of Biology

Grant Ramsey

KU Leuven

Grant Ramsey is a BOFZAP research professor at the Institute of Philosophy, KU Leuven, Belgium. His work centers on philosophical problems at the foundation of evolutionary biology. He has been awarded the Popper Prize twice for his work in this area. He also publishes in the philosophy of animal behavior, human nature and the moral emotions. He runs the Ramsey Lab (theramseylab.org), a highly collaborative research group focused on issues in the philosophy of the life sciences.

Michael Ruse

Florida State University

Michael Ruse is the Lucyle T. Werkmeister Professor of Philosophy and the Director of the Program in the History and Philosophy of Science at Florida State University. He is Professor Emeritus at the University of Guelph, in Ontario, Canada. He is a former Guggenheim fellow and Gifford lecturer. He is the author or editor of over sixty books, most recently *Darwinism as Religion: What Literature Tells Us about Evolution*; *On Purpose*; *The Problem of War: Darwinism, Christianity, and their Battle to Understand Human Conflict*; and *A Meaning to Life*.

About the Series

This Cambridge Elements series provides concise and structured introductions to all of the central topics in the philosophy of biology. Contributors to the series are cutting-edge researchers who offer balanced, comprehensive coverage of multiple perspectives, while also developing new ideas and arguments from a unique viewpoint.

Cambridge Elements ≡

Philosophy of Biology

Elements in the Series

A full series listing is available at: www.cambridge.org/EPBY

Printed in the United States
by Baker & Taylor Publisher Services